The Gift of Bread

The
Gift of Bread

Recipes *for the* Heart and the Table

KAREN
WHITING

WORTHY®
Inspired

Library of Congress Control Number: 2017941842

For foreign and subsidiary rights, contact rights@worthypublishing.com

Published in association with the literary agency Books and Such.

ISBN: 978-1-68397-025-5 (hardcover)

Cover Design: Bruce Gore | GoreStudio.com

Printed in the United States of America

17 18 19 20 21 LBM 8 7 6 5 4 3 2 1

This book is in memory of my grandmothers,
Nora Doody and Marion Hartigan,
and my mother, Marie Hartigan.
I am grateful they taught me
to make and appreciate bread.
They also shared their faith
and showed me their generous spirits.

Contents

Introduction   1

SECTION ONE: BIBLICAL PURPOSE OF BREAD

1. The Invitation   5
2. A Special Setting for Bread   9
3. Quick Breads, Quick Relationships   13
4. Come to the Table   17
5. Bread and Relationships   21
6. The Staff of Life   27
7. Our Daily Bread   31
8. Communion   35
9. Breaking Bread Together   39
10. Unleavened Bread   43

SECTION TWO: BREAD INGREDIENTS

11. More Than a Grain of Wheat: Flour, the Hero   51
12. Yeast   55
13. Sweet Encouragement   59
14. Eggs and Bread   63
15. Liquid and Additional Rising   67
16. Oil, the Tenderizer; Salt, the Preserver   71

SECTION THREE: TYPES OF BREAD

17. Bread for All   77
18. Shaped Bread   81

19. Not By Bread Alone   85

20. Between the Slices   89

21. Cups Overflowing   93

22. Sourdough Starts   97

23. Garden Bread   101

24. Fruit Bread   105

25. Date Nut Bread   109

26. Friendship Bread   113

27. Filled with Hope   119

28. I'll Bring the Bread (Electric Touch)   123

29. Sticking Together   127

30. Bread for Angels   131

SECTION FOUR: SHARING BREAD

31. Two Loaves Are Better Than One   137

32. Bread of the Presence   141

33. Guarding Bread   145

34. Sweet Bread   149

35. Blended Together   153

SECTION FIVE: STEPS IN BREAD MAKING

36. Gather and Measure Ingredients   159

37. Dissolved   165

38. Making a Smooth Batter   169

39. Waiting for the Dough to Rise   173

40. Whack! The Necessary Punch   177

41. Kneading   181

42. Shaping the Bread   185

43. Baking to Perfection   189

SECTION SIX: CONDITIONS OF BREAD

44. Moldy Bread   195

45. Burnt Offerings   201

46. Rocky Rolls   205

47. Bread Scraps   209

48. Worse Than Stale Bread   213

49. Up with Crumbs!   217

SECTION SEVEN: BREAD FROM HEAVEN

50. Dreams of Wheat and Bread   223

51. Storing Grain   227

52. Gideon's Bread Dream and Victory   231

53. Manna from Heaven   235

SECTION EIGHT: FEASTS OF BREAD

54. Celebration with Bread   241

55. Picnic with Jesus   245

56. Worshipers with Bread   249

57. Royal Feast   253

58. Promised Long Ago   257

59. Give Thanks   261

60. Extravagant Love   265

Conclusion   269

Notes   271

Acknowledgements   273

Introduction

THIS BOOK IS AN OPEN INVITATION to enjoy breaking and sharing bread with loved ones. Reflect on the wonders of God's nurturing love revealed through His Word as you savor a satisfying slice of bread, an aromatic muffin, or a filling bagel.

Bread and its ingredients are familiar symbols throughout the Bible. These symbols reveal a threefold purpose of bread: sustenance that meets the need for nourishment, fellowship found in breaking bread together, and our covenant relationship with God (see Genesis 14:18; John 6:51).

We can see the triune nature of God in the Creator who made bread for sustenance, the Savior whose body was broken to redeem us, and the Holy Spirit, our helper who lives within us, uniting us with God and allowing us a continuing relationship based on covenant. God gave the Israelites a covenant that included bread placed on the altar, and Christ broke bread as He shared a new covenant with His disciples.

For me, faith and bread will always be linked together. Bread has always been a passion for my family and me. My grandmothers and mother taught me to bake bread. I, in turn, passed on my joy of bread making to my five children. Rebecca, James, and Darlene especially enjoy bread making while Michael and Daniel enjoy tasting the new bread recipes we bake.

It is my prayer that, as we taste and share bread together, your soul will be filled and you will feel satisfied.

Biblical Purpose of Bread

BREAD

We need the grains as food.

We break it in fellowship.

We picture it as representing our ever present God.

Discover God's purpose in using bread throughout the Bible.

CHAPTER 1

The Invitation

Jesus said to them, "I am the bread of life; he who comes to Me will not hunger, and he who believes in Me will never thirst."
JOHN 6:35

"MMM, MOM, I SMELL WHEAT BREAD. Is it ready?" Rebecca called as she rushed in from school.

"Almost." I slid four plump, golden-brown loaves from the oven.

The boys' laughter filled the air as they entered the room. James said, "I'll get the butter. I want three big slices."

"I'll pour drinks." Michael added.

The children sat around the table and waited as I sliced and buttered hot, steaming bread and offered them honey to spread on it. Finally, we started munching, and the chatter began about homework, test results, conversations with friends, and upcoming plans. As they shared the tougher moments of their day, they sighed, relaxed, and let go of problems.

It takes planning to have your bread ready at the right time, although bread machines make it easier since they have automatic timers that can be used. But when the inviting aroma of bread fills the air, it beckons people to sit and enjoy a relaxing time at the table. Nothing seems to warm hearts and open conversation as well as fresh-baked bread.

LOVIN' FROM THE LORD

So Abraham hurried into the tent to Sarah. "Quick," he said,
"get three seahs of the finest flour and knead it and bake some bread."
GENESIS 18:6 NIV

In biblical times, bread served as a vital sign of hospitality. Living in a desert meant Abraham saw few strangers, so when he looked up and saw the unexpected heavenly visitors arriving, he asked them to stay and eat. He also offered to have water brought so they could wash their feet. Abraham showed hospitality without asking the visitors why they came or where they came from.

He then ran into the tent and said to his wife, Sarah, "Get three seahs of fine flour, knead it, and bake some bread." Then Abraham picked out a choice calf, gave it to his servant, and had it grilled to go with the bread.

Sarah baked the bread from fine flour instead of coarse meal, to honor the guests. It took much longer to grind wheat into finer flour, so most of the time people used coarse meal and shaped small cakes that baked quickly. Kneading took extra time and care; she had to press and turn the dough several times to release the air bubbles and activate the yeast that would make the bread rise.

The aroma of warm bread baked in an outdoor oven filled the air. Abraham served the meat with the bread and drinks. After eating bread and enjoying the warm hospitality

---

FOOD FOR THOUGHT

Reflect on your memories of fresh-baked bread.

Remember the first time you had communion and what it meant to you.

Abraham and Sarah offered, the visitors spoke, disclosing coming joys and sorrows, including the prophecy of Isaac's birth and the news that God planned to destroy Sodom.

This is precisely how Christ welcomes us into His kingdom. Christ calls each of us, as honored guests, to eat the bread He offers. It's the best, for He offers Himself, the Bread of Life. He also beckons us to open up and share what's on our hearts when we break bread and share in communion.

When did you last enjoy fresh-baked bread? What memories do you associate with communion? Savor a slice of fresh bread or favorite variety of muffin as you read the pages of this book.

THE JOY OF BREAD MAKING

Agape is a Greek word meaning unconditional love, such as the love Christ has for us. An *agape meal* is a Christian fellowship meal.

Agape Meal Invitation

Invite friends or family for an agape meal, asking them to bring their favorite bread, rolls, or muffins to share. Also ask them to provide copies of the recipe if they plan to bring homemade bread.

Serve a variety of beverages with the bread and use your best dishes. If anyone has wheat allergies, include some gluten-free bread. Fill a small basket with Scriptures about bread, written on bread-shaped papers for guests to read and reflect upon. Light candles to give the room a warm glow. Prepare your bread to come out of the oven as guests arrive, so the aroma permeates your home.

As guests arrive, add the breads they bring to the table. Provide butter, honey, jams, and cheese to accompany the bread. Put out a bowl of grapes or other fruits. Start the gathering by giving thanks to God for the blessings of a bounty of food and great fellowship.

Ask friends to share memories of fresh-baked bread or rolls. What breads do they connect with special childhood holidays? What restaurants serve special breads they enjoy that cause them to return? Share your own memories too. Capture this time together with photos. It might become a new tradition.

An alternative would be to have a private communion with the Lord. Set a date and then, on that day, set the table with bread, grapes, and juice or wine. Place a candle on the table. Select your favorite Bible passage about bread. Relax, savor the flavor and texture of the bread, and then talk to God.

Use this quiet time for prayer and reflection. Give thanks for the blessings God has given you. Let Him know your worries and needs. Read other passages about bread. Listen to praise music. Review the words of Jesus in John 5 where He multiplied bread and then declared He is the Bread of Life. Journal as you reflect. Let God's love fill your heart and mind. Look up any Scripture passages that come to mind. Remember that God multiplies blessings and He is able to satisfy you.

A MORSEL OF BREAD

Start a day with the aroma
of fresh cinnamon toast.
Accompany it with the sweetness
of God's Word.

CHAPTER 2

A Special Setting for Bread

But as for you, Bethlehem Ephrathah, too little to be among
the clans of Judah, from you One will go forth for Me to be ruler
in Israel. His goings forth are from long ago, from the days of eternity.
MICAH 5:2

I GIVE BREAD A SPECIAL PLACE at my table, in honor of Jesus, the Bread of Life.

I have collected a variety of bread baskets for different types of bread. I have also purchased decorated napkins to cover open bread baskets. Sitting in the center of the table, each bread basket serves as a reminder of God's presence.

Think of ways to give bread a special place of honor at your table. Experiment with arranging bread, wheat, and fruits to create appealing centerpieces. Print a Scripture about bread on a small card, attach it to a skewer or place card holder, and add it to the centerpiece.

Our family made a special bread plate as a reminder of God's provision. The plate pictures a loaf of bread with hearts popping out. The words "Lovin' from the Lord!" surround the loaf. When guests remark about the plate, it opens discussion about Jesus and provides an opportunity to share our faith, inviting everyone to make room in their hearts for Him.

Beyond bringing bread to the table as a central part of meals, Christians should make Jesus, the true bread, central in their lives. Let His Word fill your spirit and nurture your soul. Let the sight and scent of bread remind you to reflect on Jesus.

LOVIN' FROM THE LORD

Now behold, Boaz came from Bethlehem and said to the reapers,
"May the LORD be with you." And they said to him,
"May the LORD bless you." Then Boaz said to his servant
who was in charge of the reapers, "Whose young woman is this?"
RUTH 2:4–5

The Moabite widow, Ruth, met her husband, Boaz, while gleaning the sheaves that fell when the harvesters gathered the wheat in his fields in Bethlehem. Boaz saw Ruth and admired how she labored for food for her widowed mother-in-law, Naomi, and herself. She didn't complain but trusted in God, whom she had come to believe in through Naomi. Ruth and Boaz married and became the great-grandparents of King David and ancestors of Jesus.

It is fascinating to know that Jesus's birth took place in a town named Bethlehem, because the

---

FOOD FOR THOUGHT

What memories do you associate with a nativity set or the biblical account of the birth of Jesus?

How do you make room for Jesus in your daily life?

---

word means "House of Bread." God deliberately chose the place and the name—it wasn't accidental that the Bread of Life was born in a town called House of Bread, a place known for the wheat that grew there. The place of His birth reflected the purpose of Jesus to provide spiritual nourishment for mankind. The prophet Micah announced the Messiah's birthplace centuries before it happened. The words of Micah gave people hope as they waited for His coming.

At the birth of Christ, the magi sought Him because of the signs they saw in the sky. They found Him because of the old prophecies that named Bethlehem as the birthplace of the Messiah.

However, at His birth, Bethlehem had no room for Jesus. His parents found only a lowly stable in which to lay Him. Today, many people reject Jesus and don't make room for Him in their lives or their hearts.

Make time to sit and relax while eating. Use the time to reflect on the day, thank God for blessings, and meditate on how He has come alongside you in the hard moments.

THE JOY OF BREAD MAKING

Create a special setting for bread at your table to provide a bountiful look.

Bread Plate
1. Buy a solid-color dinner plate and permanent, nontoxic markers.
2. Draw a colorful design of bread or wheat on the center of the plate. You might want to design on paper first or cut a stencil.
3. Write a Bible verse about bread around your design.
4. Write each family member's name on the plate.
5. Bake the plate with the design at 425 degrees for thirty minutes. Turn off the oven and let the plate cool completely. Remove from oven. Wash by hand with soapy water. You can put these decorated dishes in the dishwasher, but over time the design might get scratched up.

6. Use this bread plate as a reminder of Jesus's presence at your table and God's provision for your daily needs.

Bread Basket Cover and Design

- Embroider or use fabric paints to decorate a cloth napkin with a bread or wheat design. Add a Bible verse about bread. Use the napkin as a covering for a bread basket.
- Decorate a wicker basket by painting or stenciling bread or sheaves of wheat on the outside.

Celebrate with the Bread Container

- Fill the plate or basket with bread, crackers, or even place a small Bible on it as a reminder of Jesus, the Bread of Life.
- Fill the plate with Scripture verses related to bread and pull them out one at a time to discuss.
- When you fast, place money saved on food on the plate as an offering you will give to feed the hungry.
- Fill the plate with sandwiches. Talk about being filled by Jesus. Discuss ways to feed the hungry or make sandwiches for a homeless shelter.

A MORSEL OF BREAD

Give Jesus, the Bread of Life,
a special place in your heart.

CHAPTER 3

Quick Breads, Quick Relationships

*When the layer of dew evaporated, behold, on the surface
of the wilderness there was a fine flake-like thing, fine as the frost
on the ground. When the sons of Israel saw it, they said to
one another, "What is it?" For they did not know what it was.
And Moses said to them, "It is the bread which
the LORD has given you to eat."*

EXODUS 16:14–15

WHEN MY HUSBAND attended graduate school, I baked yeast bread from scratch every Tuesday. Every week, Ron, my husband's closest friend, would come over to study and eat bread with us.

Over the years, as our family increased to seven, I found less and less time to bake yeast bread on a steady basis. Instead, I whipped up quick-bread batters, stirring in fruits like banana, mango, or strawberries. I often used local produce. Baking soda or baking powder caused these breads to rise.

In Hawaii, we picked mangos from trees near the swimming pool. In Connecticut and Maryland, we picked wild berries; in New York, we used zucchini from the garden. In Florida, we used bananas. My children enjoyed such breads that I made so much faster without the waiting for dough to rise. They satisfied their growling stomachs.

Quick breads take a few minutes to mix and an hour in the oven. They are also easy for children to help mix and cook. The simplicity reminds me of how easily I can chat with God in prayer. Like the quick breads' cooking time, even a brief time with God results in a refreshed and nourished relationship.

One Christmas, my husband gave me an electric bread machine, and I discovered I could easily adapt my recipes to the machine. Now I can drop in the ingredients and set the machine to prepare just about any bread, including my wheat bread. Later, the smell of the baked bread greets me. The ease and speed amazes me, but never as much as the speed of a quick prayer and how quickly God responds, filling my heart with peace and joy.

LOVIN' FROM THE LORD

The house of Israel named it manna, and it was like
coriander seed, white, and its taste was like wafers with honey.
EXODUS 16:31

God provided bread easily and amazingly in many ways in the Bible, including raining bread from heaven for forty years to feed His people in the desert. The Israelites only had to wake up, walk out, and pick up bread from heaven, called manna. Since it had a honey taste, it was also naturally sweet.

The only time the people could gather extra was the day before the Sabbath. Then, they would gather enough for that day and the next day. God used the planned-leftovers to give them a day of rest and a day to recall His generosity.

God provided bread quickly at other times too. Ravens and an angel carried bread to Elijah when he felt exhausted and discouraged. Bread cakes from the angel energized Elijah enough for a forty-day journey. That's energy food at its best! And, at the Last Supper, the bread was already at the table for Jesus to share with His closest companions. He broke it and passed it around the table.

The real miracle of Jesus, the Bread of Life, is His instant availability. He's ready for anyone without purchasing, measuring, or even touching a button connected to electricity! He's as close and available as a prayer.

> **FOOD FOR THOUGHT**
>
> When have you called on Jesus and received an answer fast?
>
> When has God provided for your needs?

THE JOY OF BREAD MAKING

I enjoy making quick breads and have learned the importance of not overbeating, of testing for doneness, and other tips that make my breads moist, tender, and flavorful.

Quick Bread Tips

- Freeze peeled, old bananas for making banana bread. Thaw when you're ready to make the bread.
- Quick breads cut better when cool. They tend to crumble when hot.
- Be sure the leaven is still good. Add water to baking soda and see if it bubbles. Add vinegar to baking powder and see if it bubbles. The bubbles indicate the leaven is active enough to make the bread rise.
- Do not overmix a quick bread or muffins. Too much mixing adds too much air and creates rubbery dough. Add the liquids at once to the dry ingredients and stir until mixed. It's okay to look lumpy.

- Quick breads freeze well and last about three months.
- Roast nuts in the oven for about eight minutes before adding to bread batter. They will be crunchier.
- If you like a particular quick bread recipe, experiment with changing the fruit or vegetable. Basic fruit bread recipes can be adapted for other fruits. Banana bread recipes work fine with mango instead of banana. You may need to adapt the amount of liquid or dry ingredients as you experiment.
- Mix liquid from drained fruit with softened butter or cream cheese for a tasty spread.
- Instead of making a loaf of bread, divide the batter into muffin tins and make muffins. Decrease the cooking time as these usually cook faster.
- Soggy bread with a sunken center indicates the recipe used too much liquid. Next time, add more flour or decrease the liquids.
- Quick breads often crack on the top when baking. That's fine.
- Test for doneness by inserting a toothpick or wooden skewer in the center. It should come out clean. If dough sticks to it, continue baking.
- A coarse texture results from too much fat, so decrease the oil or butter in the recipe.
- Too much sugar results in a thick, dark crust.
- Experiment with different spices to change the flavor.
- Consider adding raisins, nuts, or chocolate chips to the batter.

A MORSEL OF BREAD

The word *companion* means "friend."
It comes from Late Latin *com panis* meaning
"one who eats bread with another."

CHAPTER 4

Come to the Table

When [Jesus] had reclined at the table with them,
He took the bread and blessed it, and breaking it, He began giving it
to them. Then their eyes were opened and they recognized Him; and
He vanished from their sight.

Luke 24:30–31

WHEN I WAS A CHILD, my family often started the day with toasted bread or warm muffins for breakfast. They warmed us up before we trudged out into the cold to wait for the bus. School lunches included sandwiches of hearty wheat bread filled with treasures of jam, meat, eggs, fish, or fresh produce.

In the evenings, I watched my dad slow his pace by buttering his toasted bread or warm muffins at dinner. He would sit back, savor the bread, and ask us about our day. For dad, a meal was as incomplete without bread as his day would have been incomplete without prayer. We celebrated victories and shared needs over bread. It slowed the meal down and stretched out our time together. My family used the time to share how God had blessed our day.

Breads nourish our bodies, just as prayer and our time with God nourish our spirits and minds. Grains provide carbohydrates, vitamins, minerals, bran, fiber, and wheat germ. Nutritionists recommend that 45 to 70 percent of our daily diet should consist of carbs because they energize us in a constant, time-released way. Sugars release the energy at once, spiking blood sugar levels. Recent scientific studies reveal that carbohydrates are the primary fuel for both the body and the brain. Whole grains are more nutritious and more flavorful.

In the same way, giving our thoughts to God in prayer slows us down and provides a smooth, constantly refreshing way to build up our souls and our relationship with Jesus. We need to spend time with the One who gave us bread, the staff of life, and Jesus, the Bread of Life.

LOVIN' FROM THE LORD

They said to one another, "Were not our hearts burning within us while He was speaking to us on the road, while He was explaining the Scriptures to us?"

LUKE 24:32

After Christ's resurrection, He walked along a road toward the town of Emmaus with two people. As they traveled together on the dusty journey, the two individuals listened to Christ explain God's Word. Finally, they arrived in town and urged the stranger they had met to stay and eat with them. They didn't want to part.

Only when they sat together and Christ broke bread did they open their hearts and recognize Him. He disappeared as surprisingly as He had appeared when they walked along the road. Satisfied and filled with bread and knowledge, the two reenergized disciples returned to Jerusalem to share their joy. They spoke to one another about how their hearts had burned within as they listened to Jesus, the Bread of Life, before He broke bread with them. They shared how they knew Jesus when they watched Him break bread. A simple sharing at the table had opened their eyes and hearts.

We come to Christ for spiritual nourishment, eager to be filled by His Spirit, eager for Him to open our hearts. In prayer and Bible study, Jesus will meet us and fill us. We can walk with Him and learn from Scripture, but we also need to take time to recognize and know Him.

> **FOOD FOR THOUGHT**
>
> When have you been excited to spend time talking about your faith with a friend?
>
> What grace do you say at meals?

As we sit and eat bread, we should pray and listen. We can leave rejoicing, eager to share what we have received and filled with spiritual nourishment to sustain us till we return again for more bread.

THE JOY OF BREAD MAKING

It's good to know some of the basic terms used in bread making. These are just a few that I tend to use more than other terms.

- *Bench* is the work surface where dough is kneaded. *Bench rest* is letting dough rest on this surface before you shape it. *Bench flour* is the flour sprinkled on the work surface.
- *Crumb* is the interior of the cooked bread or the pattern formed by tiny holes in the bread.
- *DDT* (desired dough temperature) is the ideal temperature needed for the dough to rise. It's around 75°F.
- *Elasticity* is the stretchiness of the dough, the property of the

dough that allows it to return or retract to its original position after it is stretched.

- *Gluten* is formed when flour is kneaded and hydrated. Two proteins (glutenin and gliadin) in the flour combine to make gluten. It provides the structure of the dough that causes it to be elastic yet strong.
- *Proof* (fermenting) is letting the dough rise.
- *Proofing* or *activating* the yeast is hydrating the yeast (adding it to water) and checking to see that it will work. When added to water, the yeast should start forming bubbles.
- *Retarding the dough* means to slow the fermentation (rising), usually by refrigerating it. In the refrigerator it will rise, but very slowly. Some refrigerated doughs need to be punched down if they rise too much.
- *Windowpane test* or *pull a window*. This action tests the gluten. Gently pull a small piece of dough and stretch it to a thin membrane. If it doesn't break or get holes, the dough is developed. If it does break or holes open, knead it another five minutes.
- *Yeast* is a microscopic single-cell fungus that causes fermentation to cause dough to rise.
- The recipes in this book call for standard packets (.25 ounce) of active dry yeast, and that equals 2 1/4 teaspoons yeast.

A MORSEL OF BREAD

Remember that Jesus is versatile—
He supplies our needs at any time of day,
surprising us with creative answers.

CHAPTER 5

Bread and Relationships

Take the finest flour and bake twelve loaves of bread, using two-tenths
of an ephah for each loaf. Arrange them in two stacks,
six in each stack, on the table of pure gold before the LORD.
By each stack put some pure incense as a memorial portion
to represent the bread and to be a food offering presented to the LORD.
This bread is to be set out before the LORD regularly, Sabbath after
Sabbath, on behalf of the Israelites, as a lasting covenant.

LEVITICUS 24:5–8 NIV

IN THE HALLMARK MOVIE, *The Engagement Ring*, a young woman and man choose a homemade meal to end a forty-year feud between their families. They create a wonderful dinner, complete with a basket of breads. Long Italian baguettes, round loaves, and other shapes are piled in a wicker basket. The young woman offers a toast, and when her mother grudgingly asks what they had to toast to, the daughter replies in Italian, *family*. Over and around the meal, truths are revealed and forgiveness is found to reunite them as family. Coming together brought healing. The young man and woman, each from one of the feuding families, discover their love for one another and their joy of celebrating family and sharing meals.

Togetherness at a table with bread serves as a reminder of family and the need for sustenance as well as the pleasure of talking with one another. Communication is vital to keep a relationship strong. God wants us to enjoy fellowship. He promises a lasting relationship as part of His family. He looks at us as His children and beckons us to come to Him and take part in the blessings He wants to give us. He asks us to converse with Him in prayer.

LOVIN' FROM THE LORD

But as many as received Him, to them He gave the right
to become children of God, even to those who believe in His name.

JOHN 1:12

Family! God calls us, as He did the Israelites, to be family. He wants to have a relationship with us. God made a covenant with the Israelites—He declared that He would be their God, and they agreed to follow Him. A covenant is a spiritual agreement that includes relationship. Now, He invites us to be His children. At the Last Supper, Jesus broke bread in a social way and made it a symbol of the new covenant that was about to be established through His death and resurrection. All believers are invited to be part of that covenant relationship with Jesus.

The wise men recognized Jesus as the newborn king, and God the Father calls us to recognize Jesus as

FOOD FOR THOUGHT

How is God your king?

How is Jesus present in your daily life?

our King, who is always present with us. God's presence is important. He is the King of the universe, yet He wants to be with us. That's an awesome thought.

In the Old Testament, the bread of the Presence sat on a table before God. It was a regular part of the priests' job to replace the loaves as they got stale with fresh-baked loaves. God used bread and an altar table as an illustration of His desire to forgive sins and to commune with His believers. As simply as restocking the table with fresh bread, so too, we need to refill our hearts with fresh words of love.

More than simply a pretty image, the bread represents the deep relationship between God and His people, a covenant relationship that brings us together as beloved members of God's family.

LOVIN' FROM THE OVEN

Three King's Bread is made to celebrate the visit of the wise men who recognized the kingship of Christ. The bread is baked for Twelfth Night, a celebration of the twelfth day of Christmas, also called Epiphany (which means "revelation"). The tradition dates to the twelfth or thirteenth century. It uses a French bread type of dough that is filled with nuts and dried fruits. The dough is shaped into a wreath, like a crown, and decorated. Some people use dried fruits and nuts as decoration, while others ice it and sprinkle it with colored sugars. A tiny, plastic baby may be baked into the center. When it is served, it is a reminder of Jesus our King, who chose to walk among us.

THREE KINGS BREAD

Dough Ingredients

1/4 cup warm water	6 tablespoons butter, in pieces
3 eggs, divided	3 cups plus 1 tablespoon flour
6 tablespoons whole milk	1/4 teaspoon salt
1/4 cup granulated sugar	1 package active dry yeast

Directions (Bread Machine)
1. Add ingredients to machine in order listed
2. Set machine to dough cycle and press start. This should take 1 1/2 hours
3. About 1/2 hour before dough is done, prepare the filling

Filling Ingredients

2 tablespoons sugar

1/2 teaspoon cinnamon

1/2 cup chopped nuts

3/4 cup dried mixed fruits or favorite fruit blend

1 tablespoon lemon, orange, or lime zest

Candied red cherries and/or orange peel

Toasted sliced almonds, pecans, cashews, walnuts, or other nuts

2 tablespoons unsalted butter, melted

Filling Directions

Combine the sugar and cinnamon in a small bowl. Add the nuts, mixed fruits, and citrus zest and stir to coat.

Assemble
1. Roll dough out to 20x6-inch rectangle.
2. Brush the surface of the dough with melted butter, leaving a 1/2-inch strip bare along one of the long edges.
3. Sprinkle filling on buttered section of dough. Add tiny doll, if desired.
4. Roll dough like a jellyroll, start at side with filling and work toward unbuttered side.
5. Pinch seams together and form tube into a ring around a bowl. Slit dough at 1 1/2-inch intervals around the outside edge.
6. Cover and let rise until doubled, 30–40 minutes.

Garnish Ingredients

2 tablespoons unsalted butter, melted

1/3 cup ground Planters Slivered Almonds

Red and green candied cherries

Directions

Heat oven to 350°F. After dough rises, gently press on almonds and cherries (use red cherry halves for center of flower and thin slices of green cherries around the red to form holly berries).

Bake 25–30 minutes until golden brown. Cover with foil after 15 minutes. Cool and then drizzle with glaze.

Glaze Ingredients

1 cup powdered sugar

1/2 teaspoon vanilla extract

Dash freshly grated nutmeg

Milk

Glaze Directions

Combine sugar, vanilla, and nutmeg. Stir in enough milk to reach drizzling consistency, adding one teaspoon at a time.

A MORSEL OF BREAD

Be wise like the ones who followed
the star to find the true King.
Stay focused on Jesus.

CHAPTER 6

The Staff of Life

By the sweat of your face you will eat bread, till you return
to the ground, because from it you were taken;
for you are dust, and to dust you shall return.

GENESIS 3:19

GRAIN GROWS AND the harvested kernels are crushed into flour, which is then mixed into dough. Yeast must permeate the dough and take time to rest and rise. Bread is not an instant creation. Neither are relationships. They both take time and focus.

When most of my children were teens, our home was often filled with a dozen of their friends who'd dropped in for dinner. Many had no one at home. A few of those years, my husband had no job, but we still fed everyone. I stretched meals with bread, using a recipe that would engage the teens. Each day, I prayed that God would provide enough food to feed everyone. Those visiting voiced their opinion that the home-cooked food satisfied them more than frozen meals or fast foods. They expressed thanks that we took time to sit and listen, and they shared surprise when we prayed before eating.

They also loved helping. I would toss ingredients into the bread maker and set it on the dough cycle. Two hours later, after mixing and rising, I'd pull out the dough and punch it down to rest and rise again. The teens then rolled it and shaped it to form pretzels. Others brushed oil on top and sprinkled on salt. They laughed and talked as they helped prepare the bread. Then trays of hot dough rose in the oven and cooked until golden. Through my engaging them with cooking, they felt part of the family and opened up to talk about faith.

LOVIN' FROM THE LORD

*He humbled you and let you be hungry, and fed you
with manna which you did not know,
nor did your fathers know, that He might make you
understand that man does not live by bread alone,
but man lives by everything that proceeds
out of the mouth of the LORD.*
DEUTERONOMY 8:3

Wheat stalks bend with the wind and shine like gold in the sun. It takes time to sprout, grow, and yield grain. Working and sweating for bread illustrates the need for bread to sustain life. Wheat, called the staff of life, covers more of the earth's land than any other crop. It's packed with complex carbohydrates, proteins, minerals, and vitamins; it also contains antioxidants in the seed coatings. More foods are made from wheat than any other cereal grain.

Our stomachs growl to express hunger. We get a whiff of bread and crave it to satisfy our need. God wired

FOOD FOR THOUGHT

How has God cared for you, especially in difficult times?

What do you do to get spiritual food?

us for that. He wants us to understand hunger. That way we can compare the hunger of our souls to the physical need of our bodies. The comparison helps us understand why Jesus sustains us spiritually.

El Elyon is the word used for God in Psalm 113. Verse 6 describes God with a question: "Who humbles Himself to behold the things that are in heaven and in the earth?" It depicts God as our leader, bending down to the earth. God cares enough to interact with us.

God willingly stoops to our level. Jesus walked among us. Clearly, there is no other being like Him. The writer of Psalm 4:7 states that God put gladness in his heart more than grain and wine. Food sustains life, but God, the real staff of life, creates it.

THE JOY OF BREAD MAKING

The kneading and rising of a yeast bread gives it a finer texture than a batter bread. Large, chewy pretzels are made with yeast. Here are a few tricks for using yeast that will help the bread rise properly.

Yeast Bread Tips

- Yeast expires, so check the expiration date.
- Yeast starts best when dissolved in very warm water, about 110–115°F. When you cannot keep your finger in water more than a second it is about 115°F.
- Recipes that use rapid rise yeast or self-rising flour may call for hotter water (120°F). That water will be too hot for your hand to tolerate. Use a thermometer until you can gauge the temperature.
- Water for quick (non-yeast) breads can simply be from the tap at room temperature.
- Room temperature matters for yeast and bread rising. It's best to be in a spot that is quite warm (80–85°F).
- Cover the dough during rising with a cloth towel; place bowl in a draft-free location.

- Test the dough to see if it has risen enough. Lightly poke two fingers into the dough. If the indent remains, it is ready.
- The recipes in this book use standard packets of active dry yeast. One packet (.25 ounce) equals 2 1/4 teaspoons dry yeast.
- Substituting milk for water will produce a softer crust.
- Always preheat the oven before baking bread.
- If you buy yeast in a jar, freeze it between uses to prolong the life of the yeast.
- Dissolve (or bloom) the yeast in warm water for ten minutes. If no bubbles form, either the yeast is dead or the water was too hot and killed the yeast. Don't use it, as the bread will not rise.

A MORSEL OF BREAD

Reach up to Jesus
who is bending down to you.

CHAPTER 7

Our Daily Bread

Give us this day our daily bread.

MATTHEW 6:11

CLOSE YOUR EYES AND IMAGINE bread or rolls from your favorite restaurant. . . . A server carries in a basket of piping hot bread, with the aroma trailing behind, and places it on the table. The fragrance brings smiles as the basket is passed and each person pulls out a roll or a slice of warm bread. Bread is part of what beckons you to return, whether it's cheesy hot biscuits, fluffy yeast rolls, Mediterranean flatbread, specialty breadsticks, or local fare.

There are several reasons restaurants serve bread before the meal. It's a sign of hospitality and a generous offering that can raise spirits and open wallets to tip more generously. Bread can also make people hungrier, because carbs trigger the production of insulin. The tradition of serving bread with a meal dates to taverns in medieval days that only served one meal daily. The bread helped fill stomachs and saved on the cost of the more expensive entrée of meat or fish. Today's restaurants are often known for their signature bread or rolls or for breads that reflect the type of cuisine served. It's part of the experience that welcomes us as we enter the establishment.

Hospitality focuses on the other person. It should be the norm in our homes and our churches, not simply found in restaurants. Biblical hospitality calls us to view each individual as a blessing from God. We're called to reach out and communicate, to try to make the person feel welcomed. Just as bread in a restaurant encourages people to linger, so our smiles, shared laughter, and conversation should encourage people to want to develop stronger connections with us.

LOVIN' FROM THE LORD

"I will bring a piece of bread, that you may refresh yourselves;
after that you may go on, since you have visited your servant."
And they said, "So do, as you have said."
GENESIS 18:5

Breaking bread together at meals began long ago, as seen with Abraham entertaining strangers. Fresh bread warms us and retains the aroma of the yeast and flour. In biblical times, people baked bread daily. They made just enough for the day and trusted God for the food needed the next day.

Jesus used bread in His parables and lessons because people understood the importance of it in their lives. In the Lord's Prayer, Jesus taught us to ask for our daily bread, and later He proclaimed that He is the bread we need. He is the Bread of Life. He multiplied bread for a crowd and satisfied their physical

FOOD FOR THOUGHT

What do you think when you say, "give us this day our daily bread"?

What do you do to make people you meet feel welcomed?

hunger. At the Last Supper, Jesus used bread as a sign of the new covenant and gave us the gift of communion. He understood the need for feeding both our bodies and souls. Daily bread should mean more than mere food that we consume. It should also be a reminder of our daily need for Jesus, for His providing for our lives and satisfying our souls with His love and spiritual blessings.

Examining the ingredients of bread, especially wheat and water, brings us to a deeper understanding of the character of Jesus that we'll continue to explore.

We should mindfully pray the Lord's Prayer and ask for Jesus to fill our hearts with daily spiritual bread, even as we ask Him to provide our other needs.

LOVIN' FROM THE OVEN

I've used one main wheat bread recipe for decades. It's easy, even though the rising means it will take up to four hours from start to the finished baked loaves. I can make loaves or change it up for rolls and other types of bread. The kneading is so easy that I can let children knead the bread and it still comes out great.

HONEY-OF-AN-EGG
WHOLE WHEAT BREAD

Ingredients

2 packages active dry yeast

2 cups warm water

6 eggs

2 cups milk, scalded and
    cooled till warm

1/2 cup honey

1/2 cup oil

12 cups whole wheat flour

3 teaspoons salt

Directions

In a large mixing bowl with a lid, let yeast dissolve in warm water for 10 minutes.

While yeast dissolves, break the eggs into a medium-sized mixing bowl and stir until blended. Add oil and honey. Add remaining liquids to yeast and water and stir. Add in flour and salt, a cup or two at a time, until mixture is stiff (you probably won't use all the flour at this point; save the rest for kneading).

Grease the lid of the large bowl with shortening and turn dough onto lid. Grease bowl and dump dough back into the bowl. Cover with lid and place in a warm location.

When dough has doubled (time depends on warmth and altitude, 1–2 hours), grease your fist and punch dough down in the center. Let dough rise 10 minutes more.

Dump the dough onto a floured surface and begin kneading (you can divide dough into 4 portions and knead each one separately). Knead for about five minutes until dough is elastic. Place dough into four floured and greased 9x5 inch loaf bread pans. Let bread rise for 10 minutes.

Bake at 350°F for 50 minutes.

Makes 4 loaves.

A MORSEL OF BREAD

Always look to Jesus,
the true Staff of Life,
for nourishment.

CHAPTER 8

Communion

The Lord Jesus in the night in which He was betrayed took bread;
and when He had given thanks, He broke it and said,
"This is My body, which is for you; do this in remembrance of Me."
In the same way He took the cup also after supper, saying,
"This cup is the new covenant in My blood; do this, as often as you
drink it, in remembrance of Me." For as often as you eat this bread
and drink the cup, you proclaim the Lord's death until He comes.

1 CORINTHIANS 11:23–26

BREAD IS BLESSED, broken, and shared at churches around the world. In the early days of Christianity, people gathered and broke bread together daily. Some churches still serve communion on a daily or weekly basis, while others celebrate less often. Sacramental views and interpretations of the meaning of the words of Christ differ, but at heart, it is significant and connected to the sacrifice of Jesus on the cross. The elements of bread and the fruit of the vine do not change.

Think of the first time you received communion in a church setting.

It's a unifying moment when we recall the gift Jesus gave us and His words regarding the new covenant, or new relationship, we have with God. Paul reminded people that the purpose of communion is to take time to remember what Jesus did for us. Christ wants us to remember our covenant relationship. That's a sacred promise that we will follow God and He will be our God who listens to us and cares for us. Reflect on what communion means to you.

LOVIN' FROM THE LORD

Melchizedek, who was king of Salem and also a priest of the Most High God, brought bread and wine to Abram, blessed him, and said, "May the Most High God, who made heaven and earth, bless Abram! May the Most High God, who gave you victory over your enemies, be praised!"
And Abram gave Melchizedek a tenth of all the loot he had recovered.
GENESIS 14:18–20 GNT

God strives to get people to connect the need for bread to the more lasting spiritual need of relationship to Him. God desires more than a casual relationship with us.

Abram and Lot had traveled and farmed together until their herds became too large to manage. They separated at that point, and Abram let Lot choose the portion of land he wanted. Lot chose rich, green land near the wicked city of Sodom, and eventually, he settled in the city itself. In a war of kings, warriors captured Lot. Abram went to battle to rescue his nephew and prevailed. Abram then met Melchizedek, a priest who hadn't taken part in the battle, but who reminded Abram that God had provided the victory.

FOOD FOR THOUGHT

What makes communion special?

What helps you live in peace?

This remarkable meeting is the first time we're shown the breaking of bread as part of a sacred blessing in the Bible. In this passage of Scripture, Melchizedek brings wine and bread to Abram, then praises God as the Creator of heaven and earth. Throughout the account, Melchizedek refers to God as *El Elyon or YHWH,* the Most High One, the Creator.

Abram then honors Melchizedek as a priest sent by God and gives him a tenth of all the goods he had recovered in the battle.

Later, as God established the nation of Israel, the priest offered the sacrifices and consecrated the people and the offerings.

LOVIN' FROM THE OVEN

Abraham shared bread with the ageless and wise Melchizedek. I recall when I first met my husband's grandmother and her wisdom. She gave a party to celebrate our marriage and included these yeast rolls.

GREAT GRANDMA'S VERSATILE DAILY BREAD DOUGH (GG'S DOUGH)

This simple yeast dough can be refrigerated and stored for 10 days. The dough can be divided and used in parts to make various breads. My husband's grandmother gave me this recipe when we were first married.

Ingredients

2 packages active dry yeast	1 1/2 teaspoon salt
1 cup warm water	1 cup boiling water
1 cup shortening	2 eggs, beaten
1/2 cup sugar	6–7 cups all-purpose flour

Dough Directions

Dissolve yeast in warm water for 10 minutes and set aside.

Combine shortening, sugar, and salt in large bowl. Add boiling water and stir till shortening melts. Cool to lukewarm.

Mix liquid into yeast mixture. Add eggs and blend in. Stir in enough flour to make soft dough and dump out onto floured surface.

Knead 3–5 minutes and place in greased bowl, turning to grease all sides of dough. Cover and refrigerate till needed.

Keeps up to 10 days.

Baking Directions for Loaves

Heat oven to 400°F. Take out amount of dough needed and shape into loaves. Place in greased pan and cover with a towel till doubled (about 1 hour). Bake 12–15 minutes, till brown.

Shaping and Baking Directions for Rolls

Heat oven to 400°F. The dough can be rolled into balls and placed in greased muffin tins, pressed into shaped muffin pans such as heart ones, or rolled into coils. Twist each coil a few times or form each coil into simple bow-knot rolls and place them on a greased baking sheet. Cover and let rise about 1 hour. Bake 12–15 minutes, till brown.

A MORSEL OF BREAD

Show hospitality with a welcoming
smile and greeting.
Make a point to focus attention
on the other person.

CHAPTER 9

Breaking Bread Together

Day by day continuing with one mind in the temple,
and breaking bread from house to house, they were taking their meals
together with gladness and sincerity of heart.

ACTS 2:46

WE HIKED HIGH IN THE APPALACHIAN mountains. A group of Girl Scouts, my husband, and I trekked for hours, first in sunlight, then in pouring rain. When lunchtime came, we found shelter and rolled over logs to sit on a dry spot. I pulled out homemade Irish bread from my backpack and mentioned I'd used my grandma's recipe, one used at a family restaurant. We said grace and then passed it around, each breaking off a chunk of bread.

It hit the spot and filled our grumbling bellies. We took gulps of water from our canteens as we devoured the bread. The girls looked a bit downcast as they swallowed the last crumbs. Then, my husband slowly took out another loaf of Irish bread from his pack, and everyone cheered. The surprise of a second loaf had the girls laughing and pulling out some surprise snacks hidden in their own packs. Like stone soup, we soon had a feast. One blessing can trigger a flow of generosity. Soon we continued on, the rain stopped, and the sun peeped out from behind the clouds.

Working and sharing together with unity makes such a difference in hearts and minds. We faced a higher altitude and steeper climb in the afternoon, but it seemed easier as we sang and cheered one another on. We ended the day at a campsite and spent time sharing a devotion and time of praise.

We hold special memories in our hearts to revive us at times when we feel low. I recall the first time I celebrated communion with whole loaves of bread instead of communion wafers or tiny bread cubes. There seemed such a richness and generosity of spirit in breaking off large chunks from a homemade loaf.

Breaking bread together, whether at church or in another setting, is a time of sharing that can easily become a time of praise.

LOVIN' FROM THE LORD

They were continually devoting themselves to the apostles' teaching and to fellowship, to the breaking of bread and to prayer.

ACTS 2:42

Traditionally, Pentecost was the holiday on which the Israelites commemorated the day God gave Moses the Ten Commandments and established the covenant with His people. As He prepared to ascend into heaven, Jesus told His disciples to wait for the promise of the Holy Spirit. That happened on Pentecost. The Holy Spirit descended upon them, and other people came to listen. As Peter preached, they believed, and that marvelous day ended with the baptism of three thousand new believers! That's exciting.

The very next activities of the early Christians included listening to the apostles, breaking bread together, and praying. They began reaching out and sharing the good news. The result of their unity and faith showed in wonders, signs, and miracles. They shared their possessions. Their numbers grew daily. The only activity mentioned twice in the passage is breaking bread.

> ## FOOD FOR THOUGHT
> What do you do to remember Pentecost?
>
> Do you think of communion when you are simply eating bread?

For Christians, this day commemorates the day God sent the Holy Spirit and established a new relationship with all believers. Commemorating the start of the church with the breaking of bread depicts the new covenant that Christ established at the Last Supper.

The next time you receive communion, take time to reflect on the joy and unity it inspires.

LOVIN' FROM THE OVEN

I grew up eating Irish bread at home and at my grandparents' home and restaurant. The family restaurant, now run by my cousins, bakes hundreds of loaves of Irish bread every year, especially in March.

IRISH BREAD

Ingredients

4 cups flour
4 teaspoons baking powder
1/2 teaspoon salt
1/2 cup sugar
1/2 cup margarine, in pieces

3 eggs, beaten
1 12-ounce can evaporated
   milk
2 cups raisins, covered in
   water for ten minutes

Directions

Heat oven to 350°F. Mix flour, baking powder, salt, sugar, and margarine together with your hands until crumbly. Add eggs and milk. Drain raisins and add to mixture.

Bake in large (10–12 inch) pan or cast iron skillet for 1 hour. After 45 minutes, put aluminum foil over the bread so the top won't burn.

A MORSEL OF BREAD

Making bread can be a peaceful process
as you work the dough with your hands
and wait for it to bake.

CHAPTER 10

Unleavened Bread

Therefore let us celebrate the feast, not with old leaven,
nor with the leaven of malice and wickedness,
but with the unleavened bread of sincerity and truth.

1 Corinthians 5:8

UNLEAVENED BREAD IS MADE fast and flat, like a cracker or a flatbread. In this passage, unleavened bread is compared to the presence of sincerity and truth and the lack of malice or wickedness. These traits reflect a clean heart. Often I have to turn and confess a bit of gossip, a snide remark or thought, or my own puffed pride. It's humbling, and I generally end up feeling deflated. This thought reveals a naked truth that conjures up a picture from my days as a young mother.

A neighbor in New York who had also grown up in New England, remarked on how I seemed to be more casual than herself, possibly stemming from having lived in Hawaii. I laughed and said I tried to take life easier than my upbringing. Then, her eyes opened as wide as saucers. I turned around to see my oldest son standing outside naked, waving his underpants, and yelling for help. I quickly added, "Well, I'm not usually that lax about things!"

I had sent my son to go to the bathroom and then allowed myself to be distracted by my neighbor. I had to swallow my pride as I went to help my son, realizing that I still needed to supervise his potty time. We discussed modesty as I gave him a snack. I apologized to my son for stepping out the front door right after he'd trotted off to the bathroom.

Pride crops up sometimes when I have good book sales, sign a new contract, note that one of my children has received an award or a new job, or other blessings. Instead of thanking God with a sincere heart, too often, I pat myself on the back. This is something I must consciously address as I start and end my days with prayer. I want to maintain an attitude of gratitude that all I have comes from God. I strive for a heart of unleavened sincerity.

LOVIN' FROM THE LORD

When He had taken some bread and given thanks, He broke it
and gave it to them, saying, "This is My body which is given for you;
do this in remembrance of Me." And in the same way He took the cup
after they had eaten, saying, "This cup which is poured out for you
is the new covenant in My blood."

LUKE 22:19–20

Jesus celebrated the Passover just before His death. That meant He used unleavened bread that He blessed, broke, and shared. The Hebrew people called the unleavened bread the "bread of affliction." It serves as a reminder of the days of slavery in Egypt. God gave them the Passover to remember the covenant made with Moses and the Israelites.

Jesus turned the traditional Passover upside down with His words and actions. The cup represented a new covenant, as predicted in Jeremiah 31. God said He would give them a new covenant written on their hearts instead of laws on stone tablets. Jesus began the change with giving thanks over bread and wine, from the produce of the land rather than the sacrifice of animals. He became the living sacrifice the next day when He shed His blood for us as He died on the cross.

He wants us to change, not because of laws and fear but because of grace and love. Whenever you break bread, recall His words as a call to a covenant relationship and let His love fill your heart.

FOOD FOR THOUGHT

How have you responded to Jesus and His call to relationship with Him?

How has God helped or comforted you during times of affliction?

LOVIN' FROM THE OVEN

The Jews didn't have time to let bread rise as they escaped Egypt. So, in celebrating that event in Passover, they use matzo bread. To be sure no leavening occurs, the matzo must be prepared in eighteen minutes or less from the time the liquid is added. Matzo is eaten for seven days and may be used in a variety of ways, including pizza and pancakes.

MATZO BREAD

Ingredients

    3 cups unsifted, unbleached flour

    1 cup water

Directions

Preheat oven to 350°F. Place the flour on a surface and slowly add water. Knead mixture until dough becomes firm. Divide the dough into 6 equal portions and press into balls, then roll each into a 6 1/2-inch circle. Prick each circle on one side with a fork.

Bake on ungreased cookie sheet for 6 minutes, then turn over and bake 2 more minutes.

MATZO BREAD
USING MATZO CAKE MEAL

Ingredients

> 3 1/2 cups water
>
> 7 cups matzo cake meal

Directions

Heat oven to 350°F. In large bowl, mix water with enough cake meal to form a very stiff dough. Spread remaining cake meal on work surface (marble or glass is best to keep kosher).

Continue kneading until dough is smooth (3-4 minutes). Divide dough into 12 equal portions, then roll each portion into a 6 1/2-inch circle. Prick each circle on one side with fork. Bake on ungreased cookie sheet for 6 minutes, then turn over and bake 2 more minutes.

Facts about Matzo, the Unleavened Bread

Matzo is central to the Seder meal that is part of the Passover celebration. It must be made in a way that meets strict kosher requirements. Matzo must be made without yeast with specially processed flour. The unbleached flour is watched from the time it is reaped; no water is allowed to touch the stalks of wheat. Water used in the baking process must sit for twenty-four hours, uncontaminated by any foreign element. Timing is important too. All the mixing, kneading on one side, shaping, and piercing of holes must be completed in eighteen minutes so there's no time for rising.

During the Seder, participants read Ha Lachma Anya from the Haggadah, a book that retells the Passover story. Here is the text that is read as the matzo is broken before it is eaten.

This is the bread of affliction, the poor bread that our ancestors ate in the land of Egypt. Let all who are hungry come and eat. Let all who are in want share the hope of Passover. This year we celebrate here. Next year in the land of Israel. Now we are still servants. Next year may all be free.

A MORSEL OF BREAD

Let your heart be pure—
ask for forgiveness;
remove any leaven of sin.

Bread Ingredients

Jesus compared Himself to a grain of wheat. If we study wheat and other ingredients in bread, we discover more characteristics of Jesus.

CHAPTER 11

More Than a Grain of Wheat: Flour, the Hero

Truly, truly, I say to you, unless a grain of wheat falls into the earth and dies, it remains alone; but if it dies, it bears much fruit.

JOHN 12:24

GRAIN, AND THE FLOUR ground from it, is the main ingredient in bread. Grain can be a symbol of our deep desire for a relationship with the Lord because, like grain in bread, we need to be sure that Jesus is plentiful in our lives.

Regular measuring spoons and small measuring cups easily hold all the ingredients for bread—except the grain. Large, four-cup measuring cups are better for measuring flour. The larger canisters we use to store flour also illustrate the need for plenty. When settlers founded America, their first actions included planting grain and building gristmills. They could survive on grain and water.

George Washington, besides being the commander-in-chief for the American Revolution and our first president, was a passionate farmer and a devout follower of Christ. He built a gristmill that churned out five to eight thousand pounds of flour and cornmeal daily—plenty to feed his family, the workers, a multitude of visitors, and still make a living from the leftover grain. He constructed the mill so the millstones were inside, thus protecting the huge sixteen-foot-diameter wheel from erosion and damage from wind and rain. He used more efficient wheels that took advantage of gravity. His French-made wheel produced fine flour. His burrstone wheel ground corn, barley, and oats into coarser meal.

Washington focused on the milling as intently as any of his other tasks because he believed in putting Colossians 3:23–24 into practice, working wholeheartedly for the Lord in every endeavor. In one of his speeches, he declared, "Make sure you are doing what God wants you to do—then do it with all your strength."[1] Like him, our focus, whether it's while we're making bread or tackling our everyday jobs, should be on God.

LOVIN' FROM THE LORD

And [Paul] took food and was strengthened.

ACTS 9:19

Have you ever needed glue to fix something or wished for a hero to put the pieces of your life back together? That's what gluten in wheat does for bread—and it's what Jesus does for us.

Jesus said that He, like a grain of wheat, must be buried and die in order to bear fruit. That illustrated that He would die to give us life. Wheat is called the staff of life, and Jesus is the staff of eternal life.

Gluten holds the dough together yet is elastic enough to allow bread to rise. Jesus offers Himself as glue, a permanent fixative. Just as gluten needs to be developed by stirring and mixing flour with other ingredients, we need to involve Jesus in our lives to release His cohesive power.

Along with bread, wheat is also used to make flour, cereals, and pastas. Jesus is also flexible with the right help for any circumstance. As in allowing bread to rise, He is elastic enough to allow us to grow. Flour provides strength and energy through vitamins, minerals, and carbohydrates. Jesus provides strength for daily living, released through prayer and Scripture.

Flour, measured by numerous cupfuls, reminds us we need Jesus in abundance. A dash of prayer here or there and a weekly hour at church is not enough. We need the full measure of Jesus in our lives! Americans eat only one to two thirds of their recommended servings of grains. They also fall short in daily spiritual nourishment. Our spiritual fullness should include prayer, praise, worship, Christian music, fellowship, and God's Word.

> **FOOD FOR THOUGHT**
>
> How do you feed your soul?
>
> How can you bless others with the breads and other foods you are making?

THE JOY OF BREAD MAKING

Types of Flour

There are many types of flour; this list covers only a few of them.

- *All-purpose flour* may be bleached or unbleached. Bleached flour is chemically treated.
- *Almond flour* is gluten free. It can be swapped fairly easily for non-yeast bread recipes. For bread, you'll need to experiment more and add other ingredients that will allow the bread to rise, such as xanthum gum or potato starch.

- *Barley flour* contains some gluten. It has a mild, nutty flavor and contains fewer calories than wheat flours. For yeast-bread recipes, only switch out a quarter of the required flour, as there's not enough gluten for it to rise.
- *Bread flour* is made from hard, high-protein wheat, so it is heavier and stronger than all-purpose flour. It's a good choice for yeast breads, especially ones made in a bread machine.
- *Self-rising flour* has baking powder in it. It's good for muffins and cakes. No other leavening is needed in recipes that use self-rising flour.
- *Spelt flour* contains gluten and is from the wheat family, but it is easier for some people to digest than whole wheat. It can be substituted for wheat flour.
- *Whole wheat flour* is made from the whole kernel of wheat and contains a high gluten level; it is good for making breads.
- *Cornmeal* has no gluten, so it is used in quick breads and muffins. It is made from corn that has been ground.

A MORSEL OF BREAD

Making bread for someone is a gift of love.
Pray for the recipient as you make the bread.

CHAPTER 12

Yeast

He spoke another parable to them,
"The kingdom of heaven is like leaven, which a woman took
and hid in three pecks of flour until it was all leavened."
MATTHEW 13:33

YEAST CAUSES DIFFERENT REACTIONS, and Jesus pointed this out two different ways, once with a reference to heaven (Matthew 13:33) and once to the sin of the Pharisees (Mark 8:15). This puzzled my son, James, who wanted to understand the difference. We experimented with yeast and other leavening to illustrate the properties of yeast, to see how it caused bread to rise, and how it caused fermentation to produce alcohol. Our experiments intrigued him so much that he did a science fair project on yeast.

One classic experiment ends with using the yeast that bubbles to make Sally Lunn bread. James mixed one-fourth cup sugar and one package of yeast and stirred in one-fourth cup warm water. He watched and noticed how soon bubbles started forming. He then added the rest of the ingredients of the recipe and baked it. When he cut the bread, he observed that it looked much larger than the dough he'd placed in the oven. It looked like a sponge with little bubbles. The yeast had caused the bread to rise.

Sacrifices on the altar used unleavened bread that was considered to be pure and uncorrupted. The reference to the sin of the Pharisees referred to the fermentation and corruption caused by sin and unbelief.

In Biblical days the yeast was actually in a starter lump, similar to sourdough starter. The reference to the spreading of the kingdom of heaven referred to the process of how a little bit of starter spread everywhere to cause bread to rise. Christianity began small and spread throughout the world.

> **FOOD FOR THOUGHT**
>
> How has your faith made a difference in your life?
>
> How can you integrate your faith into every aspect of your life the way yeast is mixed with flour to make bread?

LOVIN' FROM THE LORD

Blessed be the God and Father of our Lord Jesus Christ,
who according to His great mercy has caused us
to be born again to a living hope through the resurrection
of Jesus Christ from the dead .

1 PETER 1:3

Yeast bubbles up to make a difference in bread making; it causes the heavy flour to rise. Looking at a simple spoonful of yeast, it seems impossible that it could lift a bowlful of flour and cause it to expand and double. In life, as in cooking, mixing different elements causes change. The yeast or other leavening is the prima donna in the drama of bread making. Yeast has much energy to give the performance, but the timing must be controlled carefully. Our hero, the flour, must let yeast work to give body to the bread. Yeast is powerful.

Like yeast, Jesus makes a difference in our lives. He has the power to cause us to rise up to eternal life. The timing of our lives is up to God, not us. We want to control things, but we must learn that God is in control. God numbered our days before our birth; He knows when we will enter heaven. The power of Jesus in our lives causes us to do much more than we can accomplish on our own.

He also causes joy to bubble up within us, lifting our spirits despite our circumstances.

LOVIN' FROM THE OVEN

This yeast bread is more like a batter bread than a dough that is kneaded. If you let it rise too much, it can overflow the pan when cooking. With this experiment and recipe, children, like my son James, can learn about yeast and then enjoy homemade bread.

SALLY LUNN BREAD

Ingredients

1 package active dry yeast	1/2 cup butter
1/4 cup sugar	1 teaspoon salt
1/4 cup warm water	3 eggs, beaten
1 cup hot milk	3 1/2 cups all-purpose flour

Directions

For experiment, mix the yeast, sugar, and warm water; let sit at least ten minutes and watch it start to bubble; smell the mixture. That's the power of yeast beginning to act.

Mix hot milk, butter, and salt in a bowl and cool to lukewarm. Stir in yeast mixture, then add in eggs. Beat mixture, gradually adding in flour. Cover with a towel and let rise, 30 to 60 minutes, until it rises. Pour mixture into a greased 9x5 loaf pan. Cover and let rise 30 minutes or until doubled in bulk.

Bake at 350°F for 50 minutes.

A MORSEL OF BREAD

Be thankful that the Bread of Life
offers you everlasting life.

CHAPTER 13

Sweet Encouragement

[The judgments of the Lord] are more desirable than gold,
yes, than much fine gold; sweeter also than honey
and the drippings of the honeycomb.

PSALM 19:9–10

MY CHILDHOOD FRIEND Barbara's father was a beekeeper. We often strolled around their home, down a hill, and past a rabbit house to beehives that hung just before a river in a woody area. Beyond the river, her dad grew strawberries, raspberries, corn, and vegetables. The bees pollinated the berries, and people commented on their sweetness. They had honey by the gallons in their home. Her mom gave her honey to eat if she had a cold because it has antifungal and antibacterial properties, plus it coats the throat to reduce soreness and coughing. Barbara's family gave away honey to visitors and friends.

Bees are amazing creatures. Honeybees provide many benefits, from pollenating flowers to producing useful food. One hive might contain sixty thousand bees, and one bee might visit two thousand flowers in a day. Ten thousand bees produce one pound of honey, so it's liquid gold.

No wonder God promised His children a land of milk and honey. Honey is often used in Scripture to represent riches, luxury, and fulfillment (see Deuteronomy 8:8; 27:3; Ezekiel 27:17). God's Word is sweeter than honey and more beneficial. It improves our minds, refreshes us, and keeps our souls healthy.

LOVIN' FROM THE LORD

This is the bread which comes down out of heaven,
so that one may eat of it and not die.
JOHN 6:50

The sweeteners in bread are usually sugar or honey. God's Word is the sweetener in life. Jesus is the Word, for the gospel of John reminds us that "the Word became flesh" (John 1:14).

The sugar in bread dough furnishes food for the yeast, which then causes the bread to rise. A small amount is used, so it appears to make a brief appearance, but it also adds sweetness to the taste of the bread that entices us to eat more. It's powerful enough to change the flavor.

We must never underestimate the power of Jesus, the Living Word, to sweeten our lives. It's compared to the preciousness of honey, a product that takes many bees much time to make. Reading just a verse or short passage a day can impact our attitudes and hearts. Going days without Scripture can cause us to feel more downcast and pessimistic and to lose

---

FOOD FOR THOUGHT

How has following Christ
sweetened your life?

How can you be
the sweet part
of someone else's day?

---

our joy. Pause and consider how friends react when you take time to read and apply God's Word in your life. That's most likely when people notice you are different in a way they admire and discover a sweet spirit in you. Consider people who have impacted lives because they live as Christ wants them to live.

My husband served in the Coast Guard. When we attended a party with people from a ship he served on, one of the men asked me what was so different about Jim. I said it was his faith and that he read from the Bible daily. He sat and talked with me for two hours. Jim's life and attitude had impacted him powerfully.

LOVIN' FROM THE OVEN

It's fairly easy to turn any bread recipe into cinnamon and raisin bread. This recipe uses the Honey-of-an-Egg Whole Wheat Bread that appears on page 33. The bread dough is sweetened by honey. Just mix in the cinnamon, sugar, and raisins when kneading the dough. They add a sweet fragrance to the air and make the loaf a bit more festive.

CINNAMON RAISIN BREAD

Ingredients

One loaf amount (1/4 of recipe) of whole wheat bread dough (page 33)
Melted butter

2 tablespoons cinnamon
1/2 cup sugar
Raisins

Directions

Heat oven to 350°F. Roll out one loaf amount of whole wheat bread dough into a 15x12-inch rectangle. Brush dough with butter leaving a 1/2-inch strip bare along one of the long edges.

Mix cinnamon and sugar and spread evenly over buttered dough. Sprinkle on raisins.

Roll dough jellyroll style, making a 15-inch long tube. Slice tube into 1 1/2-inch pieces and turn sideways to see spiral.

Place in a greased baking dish. Cover with slightly damp towel and let rise 25 minutes. Bake 25 minutes or until bread turns golden.

Glaze

2 cups powdered sugar
Milk

Directions

Mix powdered sugar and milk with a whisk to a smooth consistency. Add a few tablespoons of milk at a time until the glaze is thick, but still flows. Glaze top of cooled cinnamon buns.

A MORSEL OF BREAD

A dried grape becomes something
wonderful when added to bread.
How do you transform others by speaking
(adding words) into their lives?

CHAPTER 14

Eggs and Bread

Jerusalem, Jerusalem, who kills the prophets and stones
those who are sent to her! How often I wanted to gather
your children together, the way a hen gathers her chicks
under her wings, and you were unwilling.

MATTHEW 23:37

WHEN I WAS YOUNG, my grandfather raised chickens and had a huge coop. I woke to the rooster crowing and hens cackling. The sounds reminded me I'd have fresh eggs for breakfast and baking.

I learned to gather eggs and be comfortable around the hens. I recall being nervous at first, fearing that they might peck me, but they mostly stayed focused on eating while we lifted out the eggs and gently placed them in our baskets. The chickens did occasionally try to peck us, a natural protective reaction to our raiding their nests. But they were more likely to peck at each other, defending their food and themselves.

So I understand when Jesus speaks of wanting to gather His people like a hen gathers her chicks. He wants to hold us close, protecting and loving us. But, alas, people can behave like the chickens. One chicken pecks another to subordinate it, thus create a "pecking order." People want to tell God what to do and how to answer prayers. We run around pecking and cackling instead of listening and learning.

I'm not around hens as much these days, but I still enjoy eggs, especially ones baked in toast cups. I still remember Jesus's lesson, too, and I try to not be like a noisy, cackling hen, but instead ask Jesus to gather me close.

LOVIN' FROM THE LORD

Or if [a father] is asked for an egg, he will not give [his son] a scorpion, will he? If you then, being evil, know how to give good gifts to your children, how much more will your heavenly Father give the Holy Spirit to those who ask Him?"

LUKE 11:12-13

The yolk and white of an egg are all closed up in a shell, just as Jesus was closed up in a tomb. When eggs open, new life emerges. The resurrection is much more miraculous, however. The stone rolled back, and Jesus walked out alive!

Jesus also contrasted an egg with a scorpion in discussing answers to prayer. The egg represented the good gifts or blessings that God the Father wants to give us. I recall when health experts first denounced eggs as unhealthy and harmful to the heart. I clung to this Scripture as proof that God considered eggs good. In fact, studies now show that eggs *are* good for us. Egg yolks contain calcium, iron, phosphorus, zinc, thiamin, B6, folate, pantothenic acid, and

---

FOOD FOR THOUGHT

How does Scripture add richness to your life?

When have you felt Jesus gathering you close to Him?

B12, plus fat-soluble components like vitamins A, D, and E, and heart-healthy omega-3 fatty acids. Lutein and zeaxanthin are antioxidants in eggs that protect eyes and lower the risk of macular degeneration.

Eggs add color and flavor to bread, giving each loaf more fullness and nutrition. We need fullness spiritually too. We need the fullness of the gospel! Christ, far more than a golden egg yolk, adds richness, depth, and spiritual nutrition to our lives.

LOVIN' FROM THE OVEN

My children enjoyed a baked egg, cooked inside toast or biscuit dough, especially on cold mornings. These are fast and easy to bake, and children can personalize the eggs with the extras they want, like bacon or cheese.

EGG TOAST CUPS

Ingredients (per cup)

1 slice bread	Chopped ham, bacon, or
Pat of butter	sausage
1 egg	Salt and pepper to taste
Shredded cheese	

Directions

Heat oven to 375°F. Trim off crusts, then roll bread slice to make it thin. Butter both sides of bread. Press bread into muffin tin or ramekin.

Bake for 5 minutes to get bread firm and help it toast; remove from oven and add filling. Sprinkle cheese and other toppings into bread cup. Dust with salt and pepper.

Drop egg on top of bread and filling. Top with another teaspoon of cheese and meat. Bake until egg is set (15–20 minutes, depending on whether you prefer a soft or hard yolk).

Variations

- Scramble the egg with a whisk and add 1 teaspoon cream if you prefer it to be more like a quiche.
- Top with chopped veggies instead of meat (tomato, pepper, mushrooms).
- Try different types of breads and cheeses to change the flavor.
- Sprinkle crumbled cereal in the bottom.
- Let each person add contents to suit their tastes.
- Top with cinnamon and sugar for a cinnamon toast egg (or add cinnamon and sugar to top side of buttered bread before pressing bread into the muffin cup).

A MORSEL OF BREAD

Consider how God
fills your heart with good things.

CHAPTER 15

Liquid and Additional Rising

"He who believes in Me, as the Scripture said, 'From his innermost being will flow rivers of living water.'" But this He spoke of the Spirit, whom those who believed in Him were to receive; for the Spirit was not yet given, because Jesus was not yet glorified.

JOHN 7:38–39

WILLIAM LISTENED TO THE RHYTHM as water from the Wepawaug River pushed against the paddle at his gristmill. The water flowed through the millrace and paddles to turn the great mill wheel. The turning wheel rotated the turbine and provided power for the gristmill. The tangy fragrance of wheat grain filled the air as William watched his sons pour the wheat berries into the hopper. The grain dropped down to the millstone, and the grinding began.

William, my ancestor, built the first gristmill in the New Haven Colony in what would be Connecticut. He and the three other men who settled the town of Milford had come to America with their families after being jailed for two years for their faith. They wanted to start a church, but they also needed to provide for their families. They chose to build a gristmill because wheat was a plentiful crop and the grain could be stored and used all year round. That mill produced grain for more than three centuries, and my father enjoyed bread made from its grain. William's desire to follow God also inspired many of his descendants to become pastors and faithful Christians.

Jesus spoke about the power of a different kind of water that only He could provide. He wants to give us the power of living water of His Holy Spirit.

LOVIN' FROM THE LORD

Whoever drinks of the water that I will give him shall never thirst;
but the water that I will give him will become in him
a well of water springing up to eternal life.

JOHN 4:14

In bread, liquids flow through the dough. Sometimes milk or cream is used; sometimes water. Baking the dough turns the liquid to steam and brings out the best in the other ingredients. The steam lifts the heavy flour and brings about the final rising to produce light, fluffy bread or muffins.

Biblical analogies to God and water power go back to the Old Testament. Isaiah 12:3 states, "You will joyously draw water from the springs of salvation." In Revelation 22, there's a description of the river of life flowing from the throne of God and the Lamb. There's also another invitation to all who are thirsty to come and drink the water of life.

FOOD FOR THOUGHT

How is Jesus a source of power in your life?

What example of faithfulness is evident in your life?

Jesus, of course, spoke of water more powerful than a moving river, a great waterfall, or the steam that powers the rising of bread. He labeled His water as living water. Jesus, the giver of water, called out and said, "If anyone is thirsty, let him come to Me and drink" (John 7:37).

LOVIN' FROM THE OVEN

Packaged mixes can make preparing food fast, especially an all-purpose baking mix, but they still need something added, especially the liquid ingredient of water. They contain flour, baking powder, shortening, salt, powdered milk, and even powdered eggs. They're good for making pancakes, biscuits, pizza dough, and many other foods.

This tasty muffin recipe comes from my friend, Judy, and includes a dollop of jam to add color and a sweet surprise.

JUDY APPLEGATE'S JEWEL MUFFINS

Ingredients

2 cups baking mix	1/4 cup raspberry preserves
2 tablespoons sugar	(or other favorite)
1/4 cup margarine, softened	Vanilla glaze
2/3 cup milk	

Directions

Heat oven to 400°F. Line 12 medium muffin cups with paper baking cups. Mix baking mix, sugar, and margarine until crumbly. Add milk and mix until dough forms, about 15 strokes. Place 1 tablespoon dough in each cup, top with 1 teaspoon preserves. Cover preserves with additional dough to nearly fill the cup. Bake until golden brown, 10–15 minutes. Immediately remove from pan. Spread with vanilla glaze while warm.

Glaze Ingredients

1/2 cup powdered sugar
1 tablespoon warm water

1/4 teaspoon vanilla

Glaze Directions

Beat together until smooth; spread over warm muffins.

APPLE STREUSEL MUFFINS

Coming up with a new recipe often just means changing up an ingredient or two in a favorite recipe. I grew up with apple trees in the backyard, and we used apples in many desserts we baked. Here's a twist on the jewel muffins above. Just substitute this apple pie filling for the preserves to create apple streusel muffins.

Filling Ingredients

1 cup apples, peeled and
    chopped
1 tablespoon sugar

1/4 teaspoon cinnamon
Dash nutmeg
Dash allspice

Directions

In microwave-safe bowl, microwave apples, sugar, and cinnamon for 2 minutes on high. Drain excess liquid. Using muffin recipe above, substitute 1 teaspoon apple pie filling for the raspberry preserves.

A MORSEL OF BREAD

Let the power of Jesus's living water
flow into your heart.
Simply ask for it.

CHAPTER 16

Oil, the Tenderizer; Salt, the Preserver

*You have loved righteousness and hated wickedness; therefore God,
Your God, has anointed You with the oil of joy above Your fellows.*

PSALM 45:7

*Every grain offering of yours, moreover, you shall season with salt,
so that the salt of the covenant of your God shall not be lacking
from your grain offering; with all your offerings you shall offer salt.*

LEVITICUS 2:13

THE SALT IN BREAD helps preserve it and keeps it fresh. It slows down
fermentation to prevent bread from going stale and absorbs moisture from
the air to leave the crust firm and not soggy. It is a natural antioxidant
that brings out the flavor in the bread and tightens gluten to strengthen
bread. These qualities reflect our Lord who has a tender heart, preserves us
eternally, adds zest to our lives, and strengthens us.

My daughter Rebecca makes salt scrubs by mixing coarse salt with oil and a sweet scent like lime or coconut to make salt scrubs. She likes using ingredients referenced in the Bible and enjoys giving the scrubs as gifts. The oil and salt combine well and are ingredients with endless uses. Salt exfoliates the skin, and oil softens it.

Sharing something excellent with eternal value is part of what we're called to do in being the salt of the earth.

LOVIN' FROM THE LORD

For thus says the LORD God of Israel, "The bowl of flour
shall not be exhausted, nor shall the jar of oil be empty,
until the day that the LORD sends rain on the face of the earth."

1 KINGS 17:14

Oil in bread helps it remain soft and tender; it also adds flavor. Eat bread made without oil, like French bread, and you'll notice it's much chewier and goes stale faster.

Oil was also used for anointing in the Bible. The name *Christ* means "Anointed One." Christ is eternal and cares for us with the tender love of a shepherd. Shepherds tenderly poured oil on sheep, especially the ears, to protect them from lice and insects that would burrow into their ear canals. Oil has become a symbol of God's blessing and protection. As Christians, we are to reach out to others with tenderness and love; we're told to anoint the sick with oil.

Handmade gifts also touch hearts. As a pastor's wife in their

> **FOOD FOR THOUGHT**
>
> What are your current needs? Have you talked to God about them?
>
> What helps you have a tender heart? What strengthens you?

new church, Rebecca chose to make infused olive oil as gifts for new friends. She simmered oil and herbs, and then let the mixture cool. She strained the oil and poured it into small jars, then added a sprig of fresh rosemary to each one. She stuck a label on each jar of infused olive oil and tied a ribbon around its neck. She made a large quantity and gave it out generously.

Rebecca's generosity reflects how God provides extravagantly. One widow turned to God for help and He sent a prophet so she would not run out of oil or flour during a drought. God provided a miracle with oil so she could bake bread for her son and her household throughout a severe drought. God understands both our earthly and eternal needs.

LOVIN' FROM THE OVEN

The Amish are known for cooking hearty meals for farming families who work hard. They burn off carbs with their labor. This Amish White Bread requires two times of rising, so set aside enough time for all the steps. It's slightly sweet, and the strong texture slices well for sandwiches.

AMISH WHITE BREAD

Ingredients

2 cups warm water, about
115°F
2/3 cup white sugar
1 1/2 tablespoons yeast
(almost 2 packages)

1 1/2 teaspoons salt
1/4 cup olive oil
6 cups flour

Directions

Place sugar and water in large bowl. Sprinkle with yeast and let it dissolve and get foamy, about 10 minutes.

Mix in salt, oil, and half the flour. Add remaining flour to form

73

a stiff dough. Dump dough onto floured surface and knead a few minutes.

Clean and grease the bowl with shortening. Place dough in greased bowl; turn dough over in bowl to coat both sides of dough. Top with damp, warm towel. Set aside in draft-free area till dough doubles (about 1 hour).

Punch dough down, then pull sides to center; wait ten minutes.

Divide dough in half and form a loaf with each half. Place loaves in greased 9x5-inch bread pans. Cover and let rise till double (30–50 minutes). Heat oven to 350°F.

Bake for 25–30 minutes. Remove from oven and brush tops with butter. Let rest 10 minutes in pans before removing from pans to cooling rack.

Makes 2 loaves.

A MORSEL OF BREAD

A soft, tender piece of bread
can give you pause
to cease from worry.

Types of Bread

People everywhere eat bread, but not all bread is the same. Different cultures have produced breads that reflect ingredients native to their regions. These breads have become associated with their heritage. Discover the joy of sampling those many types of bread. Try what's available to you—you may find yourself developing new friendships and connections through your exploration of bread.

CHAPTER 17

Bread for All

Since there is one bread, we who are many are one body;
for we all partake of the one bread.

1 CORINTHIANS 10:17

I GREW UP IN CONNECTICUT, so my culinary experience and knowledge was based on the foods of that region. My husband's family had Southern roots; his parents were from Mississippi and Georgia. When we married, rich Southern foods became part of my life. I learned to make sweet tea, fried chicken, biscuits, and Southern cornbread. My mother-in-law used special pans for cooking cornbread, including a cast-iron pan with corncob-shaped wells for the batter. She always made hers with buttermilk. The Yankee cornbread I grew up with is sweeter, with sugar added and often served with maple syrup.

My husband liked cornbread dressing at Thanksgiving while I preferred Yankee bread stuffing, so I alternated which one I made. Some of the fun of becoming part of a new family is getting to enjoy new traditions, including new breads, and the differences that reflect the history and agriculture of each region. Blending cultures is part of building relationships and strong bonds. I love getting to know people of many backgrounds and discovering new recipes. God calls us to love one another, and that starts with getting to know people.

For every land and nationality, bread is a staple. The world is full of hungry people, and many organizations try to feed them. The world is also full of people starving for love and in need of God's love.

We first reach out to someone when we discover the person and his or her needs. We build relationship by responding to those needs. That action opens hearts to becoming friends and allows you to share your faith. These steps build unity to help us truly become one in Christ.

LOVIN' FROM THE LORD

Is not the cup of blessing which we bless a sharing in the blood of Christ?
Is not the bread which we break a sharing in the body of Christ?
1 Corinthians 10:16

In this passage, Paul uses the image of communion—the sharing of the wine and bread—to remind Christians that we are to be united in Christ. I dreamed once of God showing me a wonderful, golden loaf of bread that crumbled as He said, "My people have made it bread crumbs." Too often we forget to feast on the Bread of Life, and we lose the focus of our call to peace and harmony. We need spiritual bread that reminds us to love one another.

We show love when we reach out to satisfy the needs of others. That might first be through providing for

---

FOOD FOR THOUGHT

What helps you read
Scripture daily?

When have you
really feasted
on God's Word?

---

physical needs, like giving food to a shelter or helping a neighbor in crisis with a meal. Once the physical needs are met, then we can reach out to satisfy the person's soul.

While the body needs nourishing food that sustains life, the soul needs something more.

Greater than physical hunger, there's a deeper longing for lasting bread that satisfies. In the quest to fill the need of the soul, people often feast on that which doesn't satisfy. Spirituality, apart from Jesus, is like feeding the soul empty calories that puff them up with pride but provide no real nourishment. Don't settle for less than your daily dose of Scripture and talking to Jesus.

LOVIN' FROM THE OVEN

There are many variations of cornbread, one Southern style, and one Yankee style.

SOUTHERN CORNBREAD

Ingredients

2 eggs	1 teaspoon baking soda
2 cups buttermilk	1 teaspoon salt
2 cups white cornmeal	3 tablespoons oil or lard

Directions

Heat oven to 450°F. Add lard to iron skillet and heat in oven while mixing batter.

Beat eggs and add buttermilk. In another bowl, stir cornmeal, baking soda, and salt. Add egg mixture all at once and mix until smooth. Pour hot lard into batter and mix well.

Pour mixture into heated iron skillet and bake for 20–25 minutes or just until set. Slice and serve with butter.

PEGGY SUE WELLS' SWEETHEART CORNBREAD
(YANKEE STYLE)

Ingredients

2 eggs

1 cup sour cream or yogurt

1/3 cup vegetable oil

1 8-ounce can cream-style
corn

1/2 cup honey

1 1/2 cups cornmeal

1 tablespoon baking powder

Directions

Heat oven to 425°F. In a large bowl, beat eggs. Add sour cream, oil, corn, and honey and mix well. Stir in cornmeal and baking powder until just combined.

Pour into a greased 9-inch round pan. Bake for 20–25 minutes or until bread tests done.

A MORSEL OF BREAD

We break bread and share it,
and it brings us together as one body.

CHAPTER 18

Shaped Bread

Then you shall take fine flour and bake twelve cakes with it;
two-tenths of an ephah shall be in each cake. You shall set them
in two rows, six to a row, on the pure gold table before the LORD.
LEVITICUS 24:5–6

THE ROWS OF BREAD on the altar in the temple reminded people of God's presence. In our home, we used bread to remind our children about God and prayer. We made pretzels. According to oral tradition, monks used scraps of dough cut into strips and shaped them like hands folded across the chest in prayer. The three holes represented the Trinity. At one time, pretzels were also hidden with boiled eggs at Easter. A painting from 1559, titled *The Fight Between Carnival and Lent*, depicts pretzels in the scene, sitting on a red cart with other bread.

Our children decided to vary their shapes as they rolled long tubes and twisted them together. We made crosses, hearts, and fish as other reminders about Jesus and prayer. The tasty treats appealed to the senses while also reminding us to pray. The pretzels reminded our children to pray, but they also needed to *learn* to pray.

We formed a circle, holding hands to pray together. We asked each person to state a prayer need and a praise, then asked the person to the right to pray one sentence for the need and one sentence for the praise. My husband or I would start to give them an example. We also used this method with a teen group we directed. It's a simple way to encourage prayer. Our words connect us to God.

LOVIN' FROM THE LORD

You shall put pure frankincense on each row
that it may be a memorial portion for the bread,
even an offering by fire to the LORD.
LEVITICUS 24:7

God used illustrations and aromas to make His point. The bread, baked fresh for the presence of the Lord, would have filled the air with its rich scent. Each of twelve loaves contained two-tenths of an ephah, or two omers, of flour. That's four quarts dry measure—sixteen cups or about a five-pound bag of flour. The priests baked these large, unleavened loaves once a week. They were large enough to be seen and filled the air as sensory reminders of the presence of God.

God required fine flour, so every week, the priests needed sixty pounds of finely ground flour. During the week, the milling of fine flour would have taken place as another reminder that God wants the best in His relationship with His people. Even wheat or other

---

FOOD FOR THOUGHT

How has God been extravagant in loving you?

What helps you remember that Christ is with you throughout the day?

---

grain growing in the fields served as reminders of God's presence and His provision of sunshine and rain.

God instructed the priests to set the loaves on a pure gold table—another reminder of the preciousness of relationship with Him. We should remember that prayer with God brings us into His presence, into a place of plenty with a God who is extravagant.

Let your daily bread or other grain serving become a reminder of God's presence.

LOVIN' FROM THE OVEN

This is the recipe I've used for years to make pretzels. It's easy for children to roll and shape.

BRAIDED HEART PRETZELS

Ingredients

    1 package active dry yeast

    1 1/2 cups warm water

    1 teaspoon salt

    1/2 tablespoon sugar

    4 cups flour

Topping

    1 egg, beaten

    Coarse salt

Directions

    Heat oven to 400°F. Soften yeast in water in a large bowl; add salt and sugar. Mix in flour with hands; knead to form soft dough. Do not allow dough to rise.

    Cut immediately into small pieces. Roll into ropes; form into pretzel shape. Cover cookie sheet with foil; dust with flour.

Place pretzels on cookie sheet. Brush with egg; sprinkle with coarse salt. Bake for 15 minutes.

Makes 2–4 dozen.

A MORSEL OF BREAD

Cross your arms like the pretzel shape
and rest in prayer to God.

CHAPTER 19

Not By Bread Alone

He answered and said, "It is written, 'Man shall not live on bread alone, but on every word that proceeds out of the mouth of God.'"

MATTHEW 4:4

SOMETIMES, INSTEAD OF PLACING BREAD on the bread plate at a meal, we placed slips of paper with Scriptures. We wanted to remind our children that Jesus is the bread we need even more than bread made of grain. Each person reached and pulled out a slip of paper from the plate in the center of the table, and read the verse. Then we discussed what it meant and where it was found in the Bible. This usually led to great conversations.

Eating around a table is much more than consuming food together. It's a time to talk and share what's on our hearts. Scriptures often make us think more deeply. They draw us in to discussions that matter, that go beyond what happened that day and help us show empathy for the sorrows and disappointments our companions have experienced. In delving into the Bible and all the problems people there overcame, we can encourage one another's hopes and dreams.

Savoring bread takes time, and so does good conversation. There's a transformation in mixing ingredients, baking, and seeing it become bread. There's also a transformation when we let God's Word change our hearts and bring out the best in us.

LOVIN' FROM THE LORD

After He had fasted forty days and forty nights,
He then became hungry.
MATTHEW 4:2

Jesus spent forty days fasting. He must have felt hungry and thirsty during that time. I'm sure His stomach grumbled as loud as a lion's roar. Satan came along to tempt Him and, naturally, used what Jesus lacked: food. Food is said to be the way to a man's heart, and Satan wanted Jesus's heart and soul.

Jesus used Scripture as His defense. He was armed with power from forty days of prayer. He had feasted on prayer. It's good He went off to the desert to fast rather than fasting in a garden of olive, almond, and date trees or near a vineyard. When we need time alone, it's best to choose a place without distractions or temptations. Quiet times of prayer refresh and rejuvenate us. I get reenergized and powered up when I spend a length of time simply praying—talking to God and listening to His Word and what He puts on my heart. That energizes me and makes me super productive.

Satan's temptations on top of the lack of food for such a long time must have been draining for Jesus. I

FOOD FOR THOUGHT

When have you fasted and prayed?

When has God sent someone to minister to you?

---

love that Matthew 4 ends with angels ministering to Him. That probably included bringing Him bread like the angels gave Elijah; bread baked on hot stones (1 Kings 19:6). God the Father supplied Jesus's needs after He used the sword of the Word and won the battle. Be sure to pause from the pleasures of the table to fast and pray and be filled with a feast from God's Word.

LOVIN' FROM THE OVEN

My mother enjoyed sitting at the table and talking at meals or teatime. Her fragrant ginger muffins were always a hit.

MOM'S GINGER MUFFINS

Ingredients

1/2 cup butter	1 teaspoon cinnamon
1/2 cup sugar	1 teaspoon ginger
2 eggs	1/2 teaspoon cloves
1 cup molasses	1 cup hot water (use milk
3 cups flour	for lighter-colored, fluffier
1/2 tablespoon baking powder	muffins)
1/2 teaspoon salt	

Directions

Heat oven to 375°F. Cream butter and sugar. Beat in eggs and molasses. Stir in dry ingredients. Gradually add hot water until batter is smooth.

Fill muffin cups 2/3 full. Bake 20–25 minutes for full-size muffins; about 20 minutes for mini muffins.

Makes about 18 full-size muffins or 36 mini muffins.

A MORSEL OF BREAD

For an hour a day read a Scripture
and reflect on the reading.

CHAPTER 20

Between the Slices

There is a lad here who has five barley loaves and two fish,
but what are these for so many people?
JOHN 6:9

WHEN WE LIVED IN MIAMI, our church made sandwiches to feed a large homeless community. Church members signed up to help on a rotating schedule. When our turn came, our children generally cut paper hearts and wrote *Jesus loves you* to enclose with each sandwich. One person might not have enough to feed many people, but a group can make many sandwiches. God multiplied the efforts of the few who started the ministry.

At another church, I was asked to help teens plan a menu for a food shelter and serve the food. Our menu included a sausage-egg casserole, fruit, and chocolate-chip biscuits. The first people through the line looked at the casserole and fancy biscuits with skepticism, but the teens smiled and said, "We made this just for you." They tried it, and soon people chatted about how good it tasted. The teens rotated serving and walking around talking to the people as they ate.

My son-in-law is a pastor. His church is in a tourist area and includes a homeless ministry. One day a month, they serve a free hot breakfast for anyone in the community, including tourists. The homeless line up and enjoy it. Visitors and church members come and enjoy the fellowship. These activities are about more than feeding people. They're also about making them feel welcome and taking time to sit and talk. Between the bites, helping, and handing out food, church members engage with the visitors. Look around your community for ways to reach out to feed the homeless and interact with them.

LOVIN' FROM THE LORD

Jesus then took the loaves, and having given thanks,
He distributed to those who were seated;
likewise also of the fish as much as they wanted.

JOHN 6:11

Jesus looked into faces and felt compassion for a crowd of hungry people. The disciples urged Him to send them away, complaining that they lacked the funds to pass out food to so many people. So instead, Jesus used the opportunity to show God's generosity. He took a few loaves and fish from a boy and multiplied them. He requested that the people sit to enjoy a spontaneous group picnic. The disciples passed out as much as people wanted, without measuring or allocating portions.

The moment started with one little boy who was willing to share his sack of food, but it spilled over to thousands. Jesus also used the time to talk about faith. That's when He

FOOD FOR THOUGHT

When do you enjoy fellowship within your community?

What do you do to reach out to visitors and/or homeless people?

said, "I am the bread of life." He used a miracle to reveal a great truth. He fed their bodies and offered to feed their souls.

The bounty of bread that satisfied an entire crowd of people showed God's abundant love and ability to be bread for all people.

LOVIN' FROM THE OVEN

A favorite in our family goes beyond a sandwich to crescent rolls with homemade filling. We usually use refrigerated dough, but the recipe can use any risen dough, rolled out and cut into triangles.

FILLED SANDWICH CRESCENTS

Ingredients

Chopped ham

Grated cheddar cheese

Chopped broccoli, mushrooms, or other favorite veggie

Refrigerated crescent rolls or dough cut into triangles to form

crescents

Directions

Heat oven to 400°F. Mix ham, cheese, and vegetables. Lay out the crescent roll and place a spoonful of filling at wide end. Roll up the crescent.

Bake for 8–10 minutes, until golden brown.

Tips on Making Sandwiches for the Homeless

- Check any laws in your community on feeding the homeless. It's often easier to do it through a church or organization that is already established and understands correct local processes.

- Most groups make peanut butter and jelly with peanut butter on both slices. This keeps the jelly from oozing through the bread and adds more protein.
- Of course, some homeless people might have peanut allergies, so consider making some sandwiches with luncheon meat or cheese.
- Add a snack like a homemade cookie or a piece of fruit.
- Try to serve the sandwiches while they are fresh.
- Some churches also bring jugs of water and cups to pass out drinks.

A MORSEL OF BREAD

Any time you enjoy the aroma
of fresh-baked bread, let it inspire you
to think of ways to serve others.

CHAPTER 21

Cups Overflowing

You prepare a banquet for me while my enemies watch.
You anoint my head with oil. My cup overflows.
PSALM 23:5 GW

"HEY, MOM, WHEN ARE YOU going to make those volcano cups again?"

Daniel liked my special puff pastry with a filling that overflowed. I usually made a cheesy sauce and then dumped in shrimp, crab, or chicken. I'd also add chopped mushrooms, carrots, scallions, or celery, and then pour it all into the hot pastry cups until they overflowed. Sometimes I made my own puff pastry, but I also often used the frozen variety.

Daniel did an experiment with baking soda and vinegar to understand how a volcano occurs beneath the surface of the earth to erupt with flowing lava. Around that time, we also made some "praise volcanoes." We used a small thimble, water, and an empty glass sitting in a bowl. We filled the thimble with water and poured it into the glass as we praised God for a blessing. We took turns pouring thimblefuls of water into the cup until it overflowed.

Then Daniel said, "I'd like an ice cream volcano with it overflowing my waffle cup." We made a few of those, and then I decided to create something with more nutrition. I put the ingredients together and then used a large ladle to scoop up enough cheesy shrimp filling to fill the puff pastry and overflow onto the plate. It's become a favorite food. We always laugh and feel joyful when we eat edible volcanoes.

Bread can be transformed into a container that holds appetizing treasures. The filling possibilities are endless. Imagine using it for chicken pot-pie or a sloppy joe filling. Connecting that image with a life overflowing with blessings provides a reminder that our lives really do overflow with reasons to give thanks.

LOVIN' FROM THE LORD

When those who carried the ark came into the Jordan,
and the feet of the priests carrying the ark were dipped in the edge
of the water (for the Jordan overflows all its banks all the days of harvest),
the waters which were flowing down from above stood
and rose up in one heap . . . and . . . were completely cut off . . .
while all Israel crossed on dry ground.

JOSHUA 3:15–17

A miracle took place when the Israelites entered the Promised Land. The waters had overflowed and flooded the area—yet God drew back the Jordan River, and the people passed over on dry land. God used the over-flowing waters as a joyful symbol of His power when they crossed into their homeland. It happened during the harvest season, connecting them to a promise of God's future provision. We recall those promises of abundance in many passages, especially some of the psalms.

Psalm 23 is probably the best-known psalm. Its beautiful imagery, including a banquet spread with delicious food and a cup that seems endlessly filled, provides great comfort and hope to those in need. It describes treating a guest royally by anointing with oil. Prophets only anointed kings. Oil was poured on the head of the high priest and sprinkled on the tabernacle. The pouring of oil and overflowing cups in this psalm show the generosity and bounty of God.

In the same psalm, we are also reminded that Jesus, our Good Shepherd, cares for us. We will still walk through hard times, but we know Jesus is with us. That assurance reminds us that His loving-kindness and goodness are always with us.

> **FOOD FOR THOUGHT**
>
> Can you name blessings and visualize how your cup is overflowing?
>
> When have you shared your blessings?

LOVIN' FROM THE OVEN

Overload phyllo pastry cups with a cheesy shrimp filling to make these dinner volcanoes.

SHRIMP VOLCANOES

Ingredients

2 tablespoons butter	1 cup grated cheddar cheese
3 tablespoons flour	12–16 ounces shrimp, cooked
1 tablespoon chicken bullion granules	Phyllo dough puff pastry shells (baked as directed)
2 cups milk	

Directions

Melt butter in saucepan. Blend flour and bullion into butter in saucepan. Add milk and cook on medium high until thick and bubbly.

95

Add cheese and stir till melted. Add shrimp and stir till shrimp is hot. Pour into pastry cups and serve.

Makes 6–8.

A MORSEL OF BREAD

Let your heart be a waterfall that flows joyfully to share blessings with others.

CHAPTER 22

Sourdough Starts

You shall not eat leavened bread with it; seven days you shall eat
with it unleavened bread, the bread of affliction (for you came out
of the land of Egypt in haste), so that you may remember all the days
of your life the day when you came out of the land of Egypt.
DEUTERONOMY 16:3

TEACHING MY THREE SONS to drive a standard transmission car remains high on my list of least desired activities. That each one's driving marked a new point of freedom and further growth into adult life added nothing to ease my feelings over the rough starts.

Each son, however, felt excitement mixed with a little uneasiness. They had waited for the freedom and adventure of driving for years. I taught Michael first and secretly rejoiced when the car broke down as though it, too, was not ready to accept his growing independence.

Each jerky halt as the car continued to stall and the clutch gave off smelly fumes increased my unease. After each lesson, grateful for safety, I reflected on my own shaky starts in God's work. How often, when I begin a new work under God's direction, do I start out with jolts and jerks, stalling and bumbling my way along, not knowing when to clutch or when to press the gas and move forward.

When Michael and his younger brothers finally learned to start smoothly, shift evenly, and control the vehicle, I rejoiced. It's a true bonding action of parenthood that helps us bridge into adult friendship with our children.

God, too, as a caring parent, gently instructs us and rejoices when we succeed. He knows the affliction or rough starts are for a season. We always hope seasons of affliction will be short.

LOVIN' FROM THE LORD

So the people took their dough before it was leavened,
with their kneading bowls bound up in the clothes on their shoulders.

EXODUS 12:34

When God called the Israelites out of Egypt, the women carried their starter dough with them as they fled. It's what the people ate as they left Egypt to start a new life. They left the affliction of slavery behind and looked forward to the joy of change and newness.

In colonial America, sharing a starter dough was a true act of friendship. The bread from a sour starter contains a unique flavor and smell. In the Old West, miners could locate a mining town by following the scent of sourdough.

In much the same way, we start our Christian lives with sourness. We take our sour, sinful selves to Christ to be made useful, to grow the Bread of Life in us. God takes our sour past and kneads it together with forgiveness to cause

---

FOOD FOR THOUGHT

Think about your past sour start and how God has used it in your life.

How has sharing your sour start helped others?

---

new growth. Then He helps us share it with others. It is in our sharing and witnessing to others that God can use us to bring others to Him. Sharing our sour start with others by retelling our stories can be hard, but this true act of friendship produces wonderful, eternal results.

God called unleavened bread the bread of affliction. We recall our own sour starts, our afflictions, because they're a reminder of how God has worked in our lives. He uses that past for our good, to make us stronger and better Christians.

Like teaching someone to drive, both teaching bread making and sharing our difficult starts make us stronger and develop lasting bonds.

LOVIN' FROM THE OVEN

My new friend Nancy Filippo shared how her late husband Charles kept his starter going for thirty years. He made bread every five days and gave one of the three loaves to someone he thought might enjoy or need it. He and his wife Nancy called this the "Third Loaf Award."

CHARLES FLIPPO'S POTATO FLAKE SOURDOUGH BREAD

Starter Ingredients

3 tablespoons instant mashed potato flakes

1 cup warm water
1/2 cup sugar

Directions

Put all ingredients in a glass quart jar. Shake well and leave lid ajar. After 24 hours, store in refrigerator, with jar lid screwed on.

Every 5 days, either use 1 cup to make bread (recipe below) or dispose of 1 cup. Feed remaining ingredients in jar with the three original starter ingredients (listed above). After 24 hours, store new mixture in refrigerator, tightly covered.

SOURDOUGH BREAD

Ingredients

6 cups bread flour

1 tablespoon salt

1/3 cup sugar

1 tablespoon yeast

1/2 cup oil

1 1/2 cups water

1 cup starter

Note: two packages yeast = 4 1/2 teaspoons. You can open two packages and measure the yeast.

Directions

Stir ingredients together to make a soft dough. Knead 5 minutes and place in bowl greased with shortening. Cover and let rise 4 hours.

Knead and shape into 3 loaves.

Bake at 325°F for 35 minutes.

A MORSEL OF BREAD

If you've had a hard start with someone,
gently nurture the relationship to transform
the sourness into something good,
like sourdough bread.

CHAPTER 23

Garden Bread

Abigail hurried and took two hundred loaves of bread
and two jugs of wine and five sheep already prepared
and five measures of roasted grain and a hundred clusters of raisins
and two hundred cakes of figs, and loaded them on donkeys.

1 Samuel 25:18

A GARDEN LIKE ABIGAIL'S can overflow with all sorts of healthy produce. As a child, I'd helped my mom garden, but I'd never planted or fertilized. As an adult, I had much to learn.

God blessed me with neighbors who knew how to garden. In Michigan, we shared community garden plots. Neighbors assisted me and advised. My pea pods sprouted and produced a good harvest. My eighteen-month old-daughter toddled along with a bucket of water. She picked the pea pods, dunked them in water, munched, and chattered about how she helped grow peas.

In New York, I shared a backyard in military housing with a horticulturist. We planted in plots that lay between cannon mounts and sixteen-inch-thick brick walls built before the American Revolution. The bricks heated up during sunlight hours and kept the soil warm at night. We harvested through the end of November. My paring knife looked like a toy next to the one- and two-foot long carrots and cucumbers we grew . . . but our zucchini took the prize.

We were drowning in the green squash. We baked bread and muffins, cooked it with meals, and gave it to friends. My daughter said, "Mom, let's have a bread stand." My neighbor's children and mine baked and sold a tableful of bread every day for several weeks. Every sale included a free box of produce for customers to enjoy. Our pumpkin and zucchini patches became the destination for school field trips on our tiny island. Visiting children picked produce.

Our children enjoyed giving produce they helped grow to others. They learned how blessed it is to give.

LOVIN' FROM THE LORD

*"Shall I [Nabal] then take my bread and my water
and my meat that I have slaughtered for my shearers,
and give it to men whose origin I do not know?*

I SAMUEL 25:11

Abigail understood men and knew how to appease their anger. When David asked her husband Nabal for food on a festive day and he refused, it nearly started a battle. But Abigail listened as one of her men explained how David and his men had protected them and the fields for days. He added that David's men now planned to attack them because of Nabal's actions. Swiftly, Abigail saddled up the donkeys and filled them with food for David's army. She

FOOD FOR THOUGHT

When have you appeased someone with food?

What helps you be generous?

packed up a feast of bread, mutton, figs, and wine. She rode in front of her gifts, approached David, bowed, and begged for mercy and forgiveness.

Her words and actions moved David. The generosity of wholesome food touched his heart and lessened his anger. He praised God and Abigail and spared her, as well as Nabal and his workers. When Abigail told Nabal about her actions, God turned his heart to stone and he died.

When David learned Nabal had died, he proposed to Abigail and married her. Abigail's overflowing garden and pastures reflected her generous heart.

LOVIN' FROM THE OVEN

My friend Judy lived on the island where we grew our bountiful garden. We often gave her zucchini and other produce. She gave me a wonderful recipe for zucchini bread that became the main one we used for the bread stand loaves and muffins.

JUDY'S ZUCCHINI BREAD

Ingredients

3 eggs	3 cups sifted flour
1 cup oil	1 teaspoon baking soda
1 1/4 cups sugar	1 teaspoon salt
2 cups grated zucchini with	3 teaspoons cinnamon
skins on	1/2 cup chopped nuts
2 teaspoons vanilla	(optional)

Directions

Heat oven to 325°F. Mix eggs, oil, sugar, zucchini, and vanilla. Mix flour and other dry ingredients, add to liquids, and stir.

Pour into 2 greased 9x5 inch loaf pans.

Bake for 75 minutes.

Makes 2 loaves.

A MORSEL OF BREAD

Walk through a farmer's market
or vegetable garden or orchard.
Reflect on God's bounty and all the ways
we can use it in our lives.

CHAPTER 24

Fruit Bread

"Celebrate the Festival of Harvest with the firstfruits of the crops
you sow in your field. Celebrate the Festival of Ingathering
at the end of the year, when you gather in your crops from the field."
EXODUS 23:16 NIV

IMAGES OF FRUIT include sweet, juicy bowls of bright colors. I grew up picking fruit all summer, starting with sour cherries in the spring and ending with apples in the fall. We harvested each crop in its season and rejoiced with the variety of tastes and baked goods we made from them.

My children loved finding new fruits to pick each time we moved. In Hawaii, we made mango bread from the mangoes we picked by the pool where we swam. In New York, we grew pumpkins and made them into pumpkin muffins and enjoyed the roasted seeds. We moved to Connecticut and used the wild blackberries growing in the yard to make pancakes. We also enjoyed apple picking and watching cider being made. In Florida, we enjoyed citrus fruits for slushies and tart-flavored breads. In Maryland, I grew strawberries and picked wild blackberries.

It's great to watch fruit grow and then use the local produce in recipes. Every fruit-producing plant has its season and time when the fruit ripens. We watch from the first blossoms through the growth cycle and then check to see when the fruit turns to its ripened color. God gave us many varieties to enjoy, and we should pause to thank Him from the first fruits of spring to the gathering of the final harvest at the end of the year.

LOVIN' FROM THE LORD

"Celebrate the Festival of Weeks with the firstfruits of the wheat harvest, and the Festival of Ingathering at the turn of the year."
EXODUS 34:22 NIV

God gave the Israelites laws while they roamed the desert. These included laws for celebrating harvest seasons, even though they traveled through sandy terrain with no garden or rich soil in sight. That's the hope of a future harvest! God declared harvest times to be national feast days. He encourages celebration. Celebrating Thanksgiving after the harvest is a modern tradition to celebrate the bounty God provides. Giving thanks changes our perspective and reminds us that the soil, seed, rain, and sunshine are all blessings God sends. Take time to thank God for His provision.

God also tied the harvest to giving and tithing. God told the people to give their first fruits as an offering Passover, the Festival of Unleavened Bread, served as a reminder of God's delivering His people from slavery in Egypt. At the Feast of Weeks, the priests lifted up wave-loaves of fine flour made with leaven before the altar. God explained in Leviticus 23:17 that

---

FOOD FOR THOUGHT

What breads are part of the traditions and celebrations in your life?

What can you give thanks to God for today?

106

the priest needed to wave these offerings in the air before God. Doing so represented the presentation of the first, small harvest to God and signaled the beginning of the harvest season.

The seven-day autumn harvest festival, called the Feast of Trumpets, included blowing trumpets. The priests gave burnt offerings and sin offerings to God during this time. This festival ended with the Day of Atonement. God called His people to celebrate these days. They were times to rejoice and give thanks.

LOVIN' FROM THE OVEN

My grandmother shared many recipes with me, including her pumpkin bread. We often used a fresh pumpkin and had to pull out the insides and cook the pumpkin before we could make the bread. We also roasted the seeds and munched on them. Sometimes we tossed them into the bread batter.

PUMPKIN BREAD

Ingredients

1 1/2 cups sugar

1 2/3 cups flour

1/2 teaspoon nutmeg

1/2 teaspoon cloves

1 teaspoon cinnamon

3/4 teaspoon salt

1/4 teaspoon baking powder

1 teaspoon baking soda

2 eggs

1 16-ounce can pumpkin

1/2 cup oil

1/2 cup nuts, raisins, or
chocolate chips (optional)

Directions

Heat oven to 350°F. Mix dry ingredients together in large bowl. Stir in eggs, pumpkin, and oil. Fold in nuts, raisins, or chips. Pour in greased 9x5 inch loaf pan and bake for 1 hour or until toothpick inserted in center comes out dry.

STRAWBERRY BREAD

Ingredients

1 1/2 cups flour

1 cup sugar

2 teaspoons cinnamon

1/2 teaspoon salt

1/2 teaspoon baking soda

2 eggs, beaten

1/2 cup oil

1 10-ounce package frozen
strawberries (sweetened,
sliced), thawed and drained
(reserve juice)

Directions

Heat oven to 350°F. Stir together flour, sugar, cinnamon, salt, and baking soda.

In larger bowl, beat together eggs, oil, and berries. Slowly stir dry ingredients into liquid ingredients. Pour into greased and floured 8x4 inch loaf pan. Bake 50–60 minutes (until toothpick comes out clean).

STRAWBERRY BUTTER

Ingredients

Reserved strawberry juice

1/2 cup unsalted butter, softened

Directions

Beat the juice into softened butter or blend in a food processor.

A MORSEL OF BREAD

Eat a fruit bread and consider how
you can be more fruitful.

CHAPTER 25

Date Nut Bread

You shall multiply the nation, you shall increase their gladness;
They will be glad in Your presence as with the gladness of harvest,
as men rejoice when they divide the spoil.

ISAIAH 9:3

THE HOT AIR BLEW ACROSS MY FACE as I carefully removed the bread from the oven and gently basted it with butter. After cooling, I removed each loaf from its pan. The whole wheat and date nut bread loaves looked plump and golden. I wrapped them and loaded them in the car with handmade clothes and sweaters. I drove to the fairgrounds and handed over each one for the various contests. I received blue ribbons for the bread and other entries. Hooray!

We celebrate our victories, sometimes with shouting or dancing. In the Old Testament, David thanked God as he celebrated a victory that way. Our abilities come from God. Since childhood I have prayed as I knitted, baked, or made things. I thank God for my talent and pray for the people who will receive what I make.

As teens, my friend Ellen and I won lots of ribbons. We stood in line as each fair opened, then raced to see what ribbons we'd won. We'd jump with joy when we spotted ribbons on any of our items. One year, Ellen even won a grand prize ribbon for her fruitcake, and I felt such joy for her. It's fun to celebrate, and we never worried about how we looked to others. At home, we shared the extras we baked with our families. But our times of celebration should also be a time we thank God for the talents and victories He's given us.

LOVIN' FROM THE LORD

[David] distributed to all the people, to all the multitude of Israel,
both to men and women, a cake of bread
and one of dates and one of raisins to each one.
Then all the people departed each to his house.

2 SAMUEL 6:19

David danced and celebrated a great victory. In his rejoicing, he handed out date and raisin cakes to each person who celebrated with him. He had a great reason to rejoice. He had fought many battles but never celebrated with such joy. His gladness surrounded the ark of God, also called the Ark of the Covenant. It held the Ten Commandments, the rod of Aaron, and a commemorative jar of manna. The Israelites had built the ark according to God's instructions, but for twenty years, the ark had remained in the house of Abinadab instead of in Jerusalem. The ark and its contents remained a special national treasure, the symbol of God's blessing and care of His people. Now, David had successfully managed to bring the ark to Jerusalem.

FOOD FOR THOUGHT

How do you praise God?

Have you ever been willing to look foolish in the eyes of others in order to worship the Lord?

Three months earlier, David had attempted to move the ark, but God struck down a man who touched it, because only a priest could touch it. David had immediately stopped transporting the ark to Jerusalem out of fear of the Lord. He temporarily placed the ark at the home of Obed-Edom. In the time since, God had blessed Obed-Edom. David accepted that as a sign of approval to finish moving the ark to Jerusalem. He prepared a special tent to hold the ark that reflected the presence of God, and then celebrated the Ark of the Covenant's safe arrival to the holy city.

However, David's wife, Michal, mocked him and said his dancing was indecent. David replied, "I am willing to act like a fool in order to show my joy in the Lord" (2 Samuel 6:21 TLB). We should be joyful when we celebrate God's presence and when we celebrate God's gift of bread. Rejoicing and praising God is always appropriate.

LOVIN' FROM THE OVEN

Date and nut trees grew and flourished in Israel. King David gave his people cakes of dates and raisins. The golden lampstand in the holy place had almond blossom designs.

Nuts add an extra crunch to bread. You can make the nuts tastier by roasting them before adding them to the batter. It deepens the flavor and keeps them crispier in the bread.

DATE NUT BREAD WITH ROASTED NUTS
Ingredients

3/4 cup shelled, chopped nuts (almonds, walnuts, or other favorite)	1/4 cup shortening
	3/4 cup boiling water
	2 eggs
1 cup chopped dates	1/2 teaspoon vanilla
1/2 teaspoon salt	1 cup sugar
1/2 tablespoon baking soda	1 1/2 cups flour

Directions

Heat oven to 350°F. Combine nuts, dates, salt, and baking soda in mixing bowl. Add shortening and boiling water. Let stand 15 minutes and stir to blend.

Beat eggs slightly, then add eggs and vanilla to mixture. Stir in sugar and flour (do not overmix). Pour into greased 9x5 inch loaf pan.

Bake 1 hour. Cool before removing from pan.

OVEN ROASTED NUTS

Directions

Heat oven to 350°F. Spread nuts on baking sheet. Roast in oven for 5 minutes. Stir and roast another three minutes.

They should darken and add a nutty aroma to the air. If needed, cook another few minutes, but keep on eye on them as they can burn. Cool on a wire rack

MICROWAVE ROASTED NUTS

Directions

Spread nuts on a microwave-safe dish. Microwave on high at 1-minute intervals, stirring after each minute, until nuts turn golden brown. Takes 4–5 minutes.

A MORSEL OF BREAD

Rejoice with a friend this week,
especially one who received good news.

CHAPTER 26

Friendship Bread

*So [Ruth] departed and went and gleaned in the field
after the reapers; and she happened to come to
the portion of the field belonging to Boaz,
who was of the family of Elimelech.*

RUTH 2:3

HAVE YOU EVER FELT LIKE RUTH, a woman with nothing but loss? Ruth received a storybook answer to a larger-than-life problem. Hardships are common in life. I've also faced economic crunches and other troubles.

When my military husband received orders to Miami, Florida, we put our house up for sale. The housing market promptly took a nose dive. Nothing sold, including our home. So Jim left for Florida without us. After several months, Jim found a house he wanted built, and we trusted God as we signed a contract. Meanwhile, I was alone in Connecticut with four growing children and a fifth on the way. In my fifth month of pregnancy, we rented an apartment, moved, and finally received a rent-to-buy offer. However, the sale fell through, and the renters destroyed the house.

The market continued falling, causing us to lower the asking price for our home by a third. Another property we owned and rented out in Maryland was also damaged by tenants and became vacant.

We finally moved into the home we had built, but within a year, Hurricane Andrew struck and destroyed half of it, although we remained safe. We tithed, prayed, and tightened the budget more. We managed to pay mortgages, utilities, and food bills. Eventually, the house in Connecticut sold at a great loss. The house in Maryland remained vacant several months before a new tenant moved in.

Through it all, we focused on God and not our circumstances. God remained faithful and blessed us financially in later years, as the tenant eventually bought the rental at a great profit for us, Jim enjoyed a lucrative second career, and all our children received college scholarships.

LOVIN' FROM THE LORD

At mealtime Boaz said to her,
"Come here, that you may eat of the bread
and dip your piece of bread in the vinegar."
So she sat beside the reapers; and he served her roasted grain,
and she ate and was satisfied and had some left.

Ruth 2:14

Ruth reminds us that God is always faithful. Ruth and her mother-in-law Naomi, both widowed, had nothing. Naomi heard that the famine in Israel had ended. She decided to return home, alone.

However, Ruth declared that Naomi's God was her God and she would go wherever Naomi went. When they reached Naomi's home, Naomi sent Ruth to glean wheat. Gleaning allowed the needy to gather leftovers during harvest time. Ruth labored all day gathering just enough to live on.

To glean means "to gather bit by bit." During a crisis, we need to glean from God's Word, hold on to hope, one day and verse at a time, and let our faith grow again.

Ruth shared the wheat she'd gleaned with Naomi. In a crisis, we can share what we receive. The landowner Boaz noticed Ruth's goodness and instructed his workers to drop wheat at her feet. In response to Boaz's generosity, Naomi instructed Ruth to seek out Boaz at the threshing floor. Kernels of grain were separated from the outside shell at the threshing floor. Here, beside a heap of the grain, Ruth lay down, uncovered Boaz's feet, and lay down by his feet. When Boaz awoke Ruth asked him to spread his covering over her. This meant she was submitting herself to him and wanted his protection (marriage). Boaz sent Ruth home with a load of grain. He asked Ruth to wait while he made preparations to marry her. As his wife, Ruth became a mother and an ancestor of Christ.

> **FOOD FOR THOUGHT**
>
> When has someone been generous to you?
>
> How do you glean wisdom from God?

The uncovering of the feet and lying at the feet is the position of a servant. It reminds us to be willing to submit to Jesus and trust that He will provide.

LOVIN' FROM THE OVEN

When Jim served at the Coast Guard Academy, we met a wonderful Christian couple, Hank and Betsy Teuton. We served with them and another couple in Officer's Christian Fellowship, developing a fellowship program for the cadets. Years later, Hank and Betsy served as the OCF staff at the academy and made bread weekly for the cadets. This is Betsy's recipe for friendship bread that uses yeast in the starter

and a mix of flours. It's a little different and less sweet than the one from Charles.

BETSY TEUTON'S
SOURDOUGH BREAD RECIPE

Starter Ingredients

1 package active dry yeast

2 cups water at room
temperature

1/2 cup warm water

2 1/2 tablespoons all-purpose
flour

2 tablespoons sugar

Directions

Mix ingredients together. Let sit out on counter for about 8 hours.

Then place starter in a closed container (like a mason jar) and keep in the refrigerator.

To "feed" starter

Feed the starter every 3–5 days (may go as long as 7 days but no longer). Use a large bowl and add the following:

Ingredients

3 tablespoons instant mashed potatoes flakes

3/4 cup sugar

1 cup very warm/hot water (from tap)

Directions

Stir thoroughly. Cover with waxed paper or lid and leave out 8–12 hours.

After 8–12 hours, stir again and take out 1 cup of mixture to make bread. Return the rest of the liquid starter mixture to the refrigerator in its closed container.

TO MAKE BREAD

Ingredients

1 cup of starter

1/3 cup sugar

1/2 cup corn oil

1 tablespoon salt

1 1/2 cups warm water

3 cups whole wheat flour

3 cups white flour or half
white and half oat flour

Directions

Mix ingredients together well. Pour small amount of oil into a large bowl and spread or wipe oil over bottom of bowl. Place dough mixture into that bowl and turn it over so dough is oiled all over. Cover and let stand 8–12 hours to rise (do not refrigerate).

After 8–12 hours, punch down and divide the dough in half. This will make two loaves. *Optional: make 3 smaller loaves or rolls instead.*

Knead each part of the dough separately by folding sides over about 12 times on a well-floured board or dough sheet to make it into a smooth oval loaf shape. Put each loaf into a greased 9x5 inch loaf bread pan (use shortening or spray)

Let rise 3 to 12 hours, depending upon heat in the room.

Bake at 350° F for 30–40 minutes.

Remove from pans and cool on a rack.

Great hot right out of the oven, but slices better once it's cooled. May be frozen.

Facts about Betsy's Bread

- A Coast Guard cadet's mom gave Betsy the starter in 1987.
- Betsy kept the same stock of starter going for twenty-five years.
- The starter was shared with dozens of friends who took it to churches in many countries.
- One friend provided fifteen gallons of honey from his hives in West Virginia to use on the bread and sweeten the ministry to cadets.

- Over a hundred loaves of bread were baked during Betsy's memorial service so that as the crowd exited the Leamy Hall Auditorium, they were engulfed in the fragrance and had the joy of feasting on Betsy's trademark bread.

- There are at least a dozen variations of the bread, ranging from cinnamon rolls to French toast to monkey bread to apple/raisin bread and so on.

A MORSEL OF BREAD

Invite a friend to a picnic with bread.
You'll enjoy nature while
nurturing friendship.

CHAPTER 27

Filled with Hope

Having said this, [Paul] took bread and gave thanks to God
in the presence of all, and he broke it and began to eat.
All of them were encouraged and they themselves also took food.

ACTS 27:35–36

WE LISTENED TO THE NEWS of the approaching storm. The weather maps showed a massive hurricane barreling toward south Florida. My husband, away on military orders in New England, left me at the helm. My older sons brought everything in from outside. The girls filled every available container with water, did laundry, and baked bread. I shopped with my toddler son for disposable diapers and other supplies.

The news outlets instructed people in our zip code to remain home so others could evacuate. Models indicated we were unlikely to be hit by high winds.

Alas, late that night I noticed the mighty gumbo-limbo trees bending in half from the powerful winds while the bulk of the storm remained offshore. I realized we'd get slammed. I moved the children and a few mattresses to my oversized closet on the second floor. All night long, we drifted in and out of sleep, prayed, read Scriptures, and listened to crashing debris hit the roof. The closet had an unusable attic access panel because a major beam went across the middle of the opening. I felt cool air but no rain, which filled me with hope that the roof remained over us.

Finally, I read the passage of Jesus calming the storm in Mark 4:35–41 and prayed. Silence reigned until my oldest son Michael said, "You should have read that one first, Mom." We laughed as his words broke the tension. We survived, although the house sustained $99,000 in damages. We lost power for four days, but enjoyed the fresh bread the girls had prepared.

The following weekend, with Jim home, we attended church. With our friends, even those who had lost their homes, we thanked God for His protection.

> **FOOD FOR THOUGHT**
>
> Has the Lord required you to throw away something in order to receive His blessing?
>
> Have you ever thanked God during or after a crisis or disaster?

LOVIN' FROM THE LORD

When they had eaten enough, they began to lighten the ship by throwing out the wheat into the sea.
ACTS 27:38

Paul sat in a boat during a powerful storm that frightened the veteran sailors. He encouraged them to eat their fill to give them strength. He also said the ship would run aground, and everyone would be saved.

Those onboard did survive, but the ship sustained great damage. They fortified themselves with bread and then tossed out wheat, some of their most precious cargo, to lighten the ship. They had tossed out other cargo earlier, but saved the wheat, the sustenance needed for life, until the last efforts to save the ship. Tossing the wheat reflected their hopelessness.

Some translations state they ate until they were filled with food or satisfied. They ate after fourteen days of not eating, so they were probably hungry and devoured lots of bread.

A meal strengthens us, and bounty depicts hope. God wants to fill us and satisfy our needs abundantly. He will provide for us during storms and be the anchor of our hope.

LOVIN' FROM THE OVEN

Make and enjoy a bounty of stuffed bread as a reminder to let God fill your heart and soul. This one-dish meal is easy to make and a family favorite.

STUFFED BREADS

Ingredients

1 pound ground beef

2–3 scallions, chopped

1 14-ounce jar pasta sauce

Pizza dough (page 126) or refrigerated French bread

1 cup shredded cheddar cheese

Directions

Heat oven to 400°F. Brown beef and scallions. Stir in sauce.

Roll dough into a large rectangle and place on greased baking sheet. Spread meat mixture along center of dough. Sprinkle cheese on top of meat. Fold both sides of dough over center, overlapping edges of dough. Sprinkle top of dough with additional cheese. Bake for 10 minutes or until golden brown.

Filling Variations
- Add zest to filling by adding favorite spices, garlic, or parsley.
- Make a chicken filling: combine cubed, cooked chicken, mayonnaise, chopped carrots, and celery.
- Fill with ham and cheese.

A MORSEL OF BREAD

Fortify yourself before a stormy day
with a morsel of bread.

CHAPTER 28

I'll Bring the Bread (Electric Touch)

What man is there among you who, when his son asks for a loaf,
will give him a stone? . . . If you then, being evil, know how to give
good gifts to your children, how much more will your Father
who is in heaven give what is good to those who ask Him!
MATTHEW 7:9, 11

MY SON JAMES GREW UP helping me make bread. It remains his favorite food. It wasn't long after he left for college that he requested I send him a bread machine and some of his favorite recipes.

His dorm had a community kitchen, and he and his dorm mates decided to pool their resources for meals. James always brought the bread. He never mentioned he was short on funds, but bread ingredients cost much less than a main dish or fresh produce. Part of his pay for his campus job came at the end of the semester, so he learned to be frugal. He bought large sacks of flour and set the machine ahead to have bread ready for mealtime. His friends loved the warm fresh bread.

He stayed at college through the summer and wanted to take a few days to visit a favorite great-aunt. He asked me what he should do to express his gratitude. I mentioned that he could take fresh-made bread. He did that and used the idea many times after when he visited people. He rang bells at Boston's Old North Church on weekends and shared bread with fellow bell ringers. When a group planned gatherings, he'd usually say, "I'll bring the bread."

The Bible speaks about generosity and gratitude. Gifts we make, including bread, become a simple way to express thanks. Investing time to make something is a way to give of our talents. Like James, the time invested might be as simple as shopping and following a recipe. The mixing and cooking might be accomplished easily with modern technology.

LOVIN' FROM THE LORD

And the tempter came and said to Him, "If You are the Son of God, command that these stones become bread."

MATTHEW 4:3

Satan tempted Jesus to turn bread into stones after Jesus spent forty days fasting in the desert. Imagine the hunger after such a long fast. A stone is dry, hard, and inedible. It cannot satisfy hunger. Jesus refused to use His power for self-gratification. In contrast, in Luke 11, Jesus stated how much more God gives the Holy Spirit to those who ask. The gifts of the Spirit will satisfy spiritual hunger. We should pray for relationship that satisfies the greater needs of the soul.

Jesus used bread when teaching about God's generosity and answers to prayer. Asking and knocking is described in two of the gospels (Matthew 7 and Luke 11). Luke's gospel elaborates where Jesus compared requests to a neighbor knocking on the door in the middle of the night to ask for bread. The man persists until he receives bread. The man asked not for himself, but to help a visiting friend. That referred to intercessory prayer.

Jesus continued the illustration. He stated that if a son asks his father for bread, the father will not give his son a stone instead. He used a few other outrageous comparisons as well, concluding with the statement that if human beings, who are selfish, choose to give good gifts to their children, then how much more we can expect our heavenly Father to give good gifts to us.

Prayer, like an electric bread maker, can bring an quick and electrifying response from God.

> ## FOOD FOR THOUGHT
>
> How have you blessed others through something that you made yourself?
>
> When has God answered prayers quickly? When have answers come more slowly?

LOVIN' FROM THE OVEN

Although I prefer to make bread by hand, I've made most of my favorite bread recipes in my electric bread maker. It saves time, and I don't have to be home while the work is done.

Bread Machine Tips
- The order in which you put the ingredients in the machine makes a difference. Generally, start with the liquid ingredients, then the sugar followed by the other dry ingredients. Place yeast in last, away from sugar, so it will not mix with the liquids and sugars that activate it until the proper time.
- Bread flour is stronger than other flours and thus tolerates the action of the machine better.

- When adding butter, cut it into small pieces to help it blend better.
- If you're using the bread machine's delay cycle and plan to hold off baking for several hours, don't use eggs, cheese, or milk, in which bacteria like to grow.
- If bread is undercooked or gummy, it didn't rise properly and the yeast or other leavening may have been too old.
- If adding in nuts or dried fruit later in the process, toss them with flour to help them blend in better.

PIZZA DOUGH

Ingredients

1 package active dry yeast	1 tablespoon sugar
3 cups bread flour	2 tablespoons olive oil
1 teaspoon salt	1 cup plus 2 tablespoons water

Directions

Place ingredients in machine in order listed. Select dough cycle, then start or use timer to start later.

When done, remove dough and place in greased bowl. Turn dough. Let rise in warm place for 30 minutes.

Knead dough lightly. Shape, place on greased pan, and add desired toppings. Bake at 400°F for 18–20 minutes until crust is brown and cheese melts.

Note: For crispier crust, bake a few minutes before adding toppings.

A MORSEL OF BREAD

There is more hunger in this world for touch,
even a quick touch, than for bread.

CHAPTER 29

Sticking Together

A man of too many friends comes to ruin,
but there is a friend who sticks closer than a brother.

PROVERBS 18:24

PIZZA CAN HELP FAMILIES and friends bond and share faith and fellowship like almost no other food. When we lived in Hawaii, we'd meet up at a pizza parlor for lunch on paydays with other families and our spouses. Family-style foods made it easy and fun for all ages to gather together. The little ones with us loved this. Our toddler Michael chewed on breadsticks that fit easily in his fist, and he stayed happy the entire time. The little ones usually ended up with sticky hands and faces—gluten in the cooked dough acts like a glue and, with chewing, softens and becomes sticky—but we'd pull out the wipes and clean them all up.

Before that move, we shared pizza with one of my husband's college buddies and his family. His wife became a dear friend.

Two of my grandsons now enjoy youth group. Of course, these groups often serve pizza that fills stomachs and gets kids smiling and bonding. It's a great opportunity to connect with believers their own age.

Through these time of food and fellowship, we can see the ability bread has to help us enjoy being together. As our relationships grow, so do the opportunities to share our faith with friends.

LOVIN' FROM THE LORD

Now it happened that He was passing through some grainfields
on a Sabbath; and His disciples were picking the heads of grain,
rubbing them in their hands, and eating the grain.

LUKE 6:1

The disciples picked the heads of grain as they walked by a field. They rubbed the heads together and then ate the grain. It made a healthy snack as they traveled. Consuming raw grain this way is similar to chewing gum.

God's law instructed farmers to leave the edges of their fields alone to provide food for travelers. The disciples stuck close to Jesus, trusting they would be fed. The basic ingredient of bread—grain—provided nourishment.

However, the action of the disciples led to an accusation from religious leaders about working on the Sabbath. Jesus responded with a reminder of David eating bread in the temple. Jesus also healed a man on a different Sabbath. He used those activities to question leaders about whether it is lawful to do good or evil on the Sabbath, to save a life or destroy it. Jesus wanted us to focus on loving others. He wanted people to understand the *intent* of the law. In Matthew 12:7, Jesus quoted from Hosea 6:6, that God desires compassion.

FOOD FOR THOUGHT

What helps you stay close to Jesus?

When have you sat with someone and bonded over bread or other food?

Jesus wants us to stick close to Him and focus on loving others with kindness.

LOVIN' FROM THE OVEN

These breadsticks are easy to make. The dough can be made in a bread machine, set to finish when you want to start shaping them. Like the grain the disciples picked, these make great snacks for when you are busy.

BREADSTICKS

Ingredients

1 cup warm water

1/4 cup oil

3 tablespoons brown sugar

3 cups bread flour

1 package active dry yeast

Topping

Melt butter and mix in minced or powdered garlic to taste

Grated parmesan cheese

Directions

For bread machine, place ingredients in order above; for making by hand, dissolve yeast in water, add the other ingredients to form sticky dough, knead until smooth.

Roll dough into an 8x15-inch rectangle. Cut strips 3/4 inch wide (8 inches long). Twist strip and place on greased baking sheet. Let rise for 20 minutes.

Bake at 375°F for 10–15 minutes. Brush with garlic butter and sprinkle with salt and/or cheese.

A MORSEL OF BREAD

Stick with Jesus,
and He will always stick with you.

CHAPTER 30

Bread for Angels

Do not forget to show hospitality to strangers,
for by this some have entertained angels without knowing it.

HEBREWS 13:2

WE MET A MAN AT CHURCH shortly before Hurricane Andrew struck our area. We chatted and realized he lived close by. The day after the storm damaged our home, with Jim still away on military orders, the man showed up to help us. He spent a few hours assisting my sons in cleaning debris from the driveway so we could get out. He also helped with other hard work. We thanked him, and my girls served him the bread they had made and water. Later, we heard that the city had condemned his apartment building, and we never saw him again. To us, God had sent an angel, and we'd offered him what we had.

Sometimes God sends us unexpected help when we need it, and sometimes He moves us to help others. In Connecticut, after Hurricane Gloria struck our street and left debris everywhere, my husband drove a van filled with Coast Guard Academy cadets who had volunteered to help with cleanup. They climbed out of the van and started knocking on doors, offering to help. They spent the day working to remove the downed trees, branches, and other debris. We fired up the grill and cooked for them. Neighbors added treats, breads, and fresh produce as thanks.

Our hearts respond with gratitude when unexpected help arrives in our times of need. God calls us to be hospitable to strangers. We don't know when they are ambassadors from God or even angels.

LOVIN' FROM THE LORD

Then the angel of the LORD put out the end of the staff
that was in his hand and touched the meat and the unleavened bread;
and fire sprang up from the rock and consumed
the meat and the unleavened bread.
Then the angel of the LORD vanished from his sight.

JUDGES 6:21

An angel sat under a tree while Gideon threshed wheat. The angel called Gideon a valiant warrior. Angels had only appeared to great leaders, like Abraham and Moses.

Gideon responded by whining, "Where are all His miracles which our fathers told us about?"

The Lord then revealed he had chosen Gideon to save his people. Gideon listed his shortcomings, "My family is the least in Manasseh, and I am the youngest in my father's house."

The Lord said, "Surely, I will be with you, and you shall defeat Midian as one man."

Then Gideon asked for a sign. He would offer bread and meat to

FOOD FOR THOUGHT

What idols do you need
to tear down?

What enemies do you
need to defeat?

the angel. The angel sent a fire to consume the offering and disappeared. Then Gideon cried in fear that he had seen the angel of the Lord. He expected to die.

The Lord assured Gideon that he would live. Gideon obeyed the Lord but also asked for two more signs. God patiently responded and then used Gideon to defeat the enemy.

How often do we doubt God's calling? How much must God nudge us and patiently wait for us to believe him? Hopefully we won't have to ask for an angel to eat bread before we trust God.

LOVIN' FROM THE OVEN

I enjoy making fun treats. Children can help make these as a simple dessert.

TOASTED ANGEL BREAD DESSERT

Paper pattern

1. Cut a square piece of paper the size of your bread.
2. Follow lines in diagram to cut a large triangle for the angel body.
3. Turn the other two triangles to form wings. Lay wings down, points out.
4. Lay body on top of wings like the example below.
5. Use pattern to cut the bread.

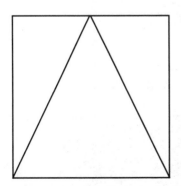

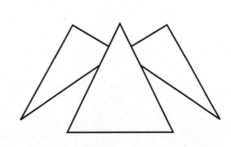

Ingredients

  5 pieces bread

  1 cup sweetened condensed milk

  Coconut

Directions

  Cut bread according to pattern, to make 5 angels.

  Spoon a few tablespoons of condensed milk on one side of bread and spread it evenly. Sprinkle bread with coconut. Bake at 350°F until bread is toasted and coconut turns light brown.

  Serve on plates, placing wings on first and adding angel body on top. Drizzle a honey halo on top.

A MORSEL OF BREAD

A pantry with bread
holds enough to entertain angels.

Sharing Bread

Through the gift of bread and the generosity of our hearts, we build relationships and bonds. The gift of bread is a sharing of time, talent, and love.

CHAPTER 31

Two Loaves Are Better Than One

You shall bring in from your dwelling places two loaves of bread
for a wave offering, made of two-tenths of an ephah; they shall be
of a fine flour, baked with leaven as first fruits to the LORD.

LEVITICUS 23:17

I HELPED GRANDMA make bread and asked, "Why do you always make at least two loaves of bread?"

She smiled. "Two loaves are better than one. There's always someone who could use a loaf of bread." Her calendar included dates circled with names that reminded her of people who had lost a loved one six months earlier or of someone's birthday.

When Grandma baked two loaves, she kept one at home for company that dropped in, and she gave the other away to bring joy to a family or lonely widow. Sometimes she baked bread in coffee cans and mailed them to missionaries. She showed her love through the work of her hands.

I have followed Grandma's generous example and given bread to many neighbors over the years. It amazes me that when I give bread away, the recipients often open up and talk. Bread satisfies hunger and seems to touch people more deeply than sweets. I bake breads at Christmas and deliver them to neighbors. When there's a crisis or death in a family, I can usually pull out a loaf I made from the freezer, thaw it, and take it by as I offer my prayers and sympathy.

Associations with bread can remain with us for years. One former young neighbor, Ben, upon entering a bakery with his mom said, "This smells like Miss Karen's bread." Jesus reminded us that when we give to someone or help the hungry, we are giving to Him (Matthew 25). Hopefully people will also associate your generosity with your faith.

LOVIN' FROM THE LORD

You shall count fifty days to the day after the seventh sabbath;
then you shall present a new grain offering to the LORD.
LEVITICUS 23:16

The Feast of First Fruits celebrates the joy of the first crop of the spring barley harvest. It's known as Hag ha-Shavuot. It takes place fifty days after Passover, on a Sunday. Hellenistic Jews called the day "Pentecost," meaning fifty. It commemorated the day God gave the Israelites the Ten Commandments. Held in late spring, it celebrated the first fruits of the barley harvest and used two loaves of leavened bread as part of the offerings. The Feast of First Fruits is the only feast that used leavened bread. Modern Jews also use leavened bread to celebrate the Sabbath.

> **FOOD FOR THOUGHT**
>
> How have you felt when someone offered you fresh-baked bread?
>
> How do God's Word and communion provide our daily bread?

Two loaves of bread, called challah, are placed on the table at Shabbat, the Hebrew word for Sabbath. The word challah means "new dough" and refers to dough presented as a gift to the Lord (according to Numbers 15:17–21).

The use of two loaves symbolizes the double portion of manna sent from God the day before the Sabbath. The double portion reminds us that God always supplies enough.

For early Christians, Pentecost commemorated the day that God sent the Holy Spirit. Some churches use leavened bread for communion since the feast day used leavened bread.

LOVIN' FROM THE OVEN

This is my daughter-in-law Mira's favorite recipe for Challah. Jewish families still commemorate the Sabbath with this bread.

CHALLAH

There are various ways to braid the Challah using three, four, or six strands. You can practice braiding with play dough.

Ingredients

1 package active dry yeast

1 3/4 cups lukewarm water

1/2 cup sugar (or honey)

1/2 cup vegetable or olive oil

2 large eggs, beaten separately

5 cups bread flour

3 1/2 cups all-purpose flour

1 tablespoon salt

Topping

1 egg, beaten

Poppy seeds or sesame seeds

Directions

In a small bowl, dissolve yeast in warm water for ten minutes. Add sugar and oil and mix well. Beat in 2 eggs, one at a time. Gradually add in bread flour. Add in 2 cups of the all-purpose flour and the salt.

Once dough sticks together and flour is mixed in, turn out onto a floured surface and knead for about 5 minutes, adding in the rest of the flour as needed until dough is smooth, glossy, and elastic (you may not need all of the remaining flour). Place dough in an oiled bowl and turn it over to cover with the oil. Cover with plastic wrap and let rise until doubled.

Punch down hard and let rise 30 more minutes.

Turn onto board and knead one or two times. Divide dough in half. Divide each half into either 3, 4, or 6 strands and braid the strands (make strands by rolling equal amounts of dough into 14-inch ropes). Before braiding, pinch the ends together. A good bread braid tutorial can be found at http://www.couldntbeparve.com.

Options: Shape dough to resemble showbread by rolling 12 tight balls and pressing them together in a greased 10x4-inch loaf pan.

Place each braided loaf on a greased baking sheet; let bread rise, uncovered, for fifty minutes.

Beat remaining egg and brush it gently over bread.

Heat oven to 400°F. Wait five minutes and brush Challah with egg again. Sprinkle with poppy seeds or sesame seeds. Bake for 10 minutes and then reduce temperature to 375°F. Bake 30 minutes. Turn off oven and let bread remain in oven five minutes to get a golden crust.

A MORSEL OF BREAD

Remember that Jesus is versatile and supplies
our needs anytime of day, surprising us
with creative answers and filling our souls.

CHAPTER 32

Bread of the Presence

*Having a golden altar of incense and the ark of the covenant covered
on all sides with gold, in which was a golden jar holding the manna,
and Aaron's rod which budded, and the tables of the covenant.*

HEBREWS 9:4

ORIGINALLY, WE USED a paper bread plate on our table as a reminder
of the presence of Jesus, the Bread of Life. Our children then wanted us
to have a fancier container. We used kits to make more permanent bread
plates and let each child design and color his or her own plate. We also
made a family plate that depicted a loaf of bread with the words of John
6:35 around it. We usually placed some form of bread on the plate, but
occasionally placed Scriptures on it instead.

When guests visited and noticed the bread plate, they often commented. One of our children quickly explained why we used it and
asked the visitor about his or her faith. It became a great way to converse
about faith.

Each evening we said grace. Decades later, as Jim faced his last days
with terminal breast cancer, he mentioned he didn't know if he had made

a difference in lives of others. That day, a college classmate e-mailed Jim. He had been our guest for dinner decades earlier and wanted Jim to know how one small action had changed his life. The friend wrote, "Forty years ago, you offered thanks to our Lord as easily as you laid a napkin in your lap. You and our Lord were close." The e-mail went on to explain that Jim's simple prayer had brought the writer back to the Lord, and he'd started praying with his wife.

Even a small prayer of thanks can reveal the presence of Jesus.

LOVIN' FROM THE LORD

I will also walk among you and be your God, and you shall be My people.
LEVITICUS 26:12

If you keep My commandments, you will abide in My love;
just as I have kept My Father's commandments and abide in His love.
JOHN 15:10

A basket of bread transforms a plain table in a restaurant to one that symbolizes bounty, hospitality, and welcome. The image of bread on a golden table in Israel symbolized a deep, covenant relationship between God and His chosen people.

In the Old Testament, God laid a foundation of relating to His people that incorporated bread. The bread of the Presence symbolized the covenant relationship. The symbolism continued with Jesus, who multiplied and broke bread when He gave us a new covenant, a new relationship with God. Bread that sustains human life reminds us of God, who sustains eternal life.

FOOD FOR THOUGHT

How is communion significant to you now?

How do you abide in God's love?

God told Moses He would walk among His people as long as they kept their word and followed His laws. Jesus said that anyone who keeps His commandments abides in His love. The covenant became a heart condition. God remains a God who wants to be with us.

When you break bread in communion—or even when you look at bread—consider the significance of it and how it illustrates the abiding love of Christ.

THE JOY OF BREAD MAKING

An eye-catching centerpiece adds a sense of beauty or charm that shows you care about making guests feel welcome. It can also become a conversation starter. Go beyond floral centerpieces and create ones from bread that symbolize the presence of God.

Centerpiece Ideas

- Bake wreaths of bread in various diameters and stack them to form a bread tree.
- Fill a vase with wheat and long breadsticks.
- Make a cornucopia of bread or fill a wicker one with rolls, wheat, and breadsticks.
- Fill a basket with grapes and bread.
- Bake a bread bowl and fill it with rolls.
- Hang a painting of bread in the kitchen or dining room.
- Fill mason jars with ingredients for making bread, decorate with gold ribbons, and place in the center of the table.
- Shape bread into an animal for a centerpiece.
- Bake small round rolls on lollipop sticks and push into a Styrofoam cone to make a bread-pop tree.
- Place a Bible in the table's center and surround it with bread and grapes.

- Fill a glass container with whipped butter and place it on the table with bread.
- Use biscotti to build a bread tower.
- Fill a clear bowl with rolls.
- Roll a paper bag into a small cornucopia, fill with a few rolls, and place in a container.
- Place muffins in a bowl to create a bouquet (place a smaller round bowl upside down inside larger bowl to help shape the bouquet) and add sparkle by basting muffins with butter and sprinkling them with colored sugars.
- Place rolls on scallop shells to create a centerpiece.
- Bake a bread wreath and place a candle in the center.
- Pile sandwich rolls on a plate.
- Place bread or rolls on a cake stand and set it on the table.
- Place long loaves of French and Italian bread in a large vase.
- Set a row of fruit breads in the center of the table.
- Press small muffins onto the ends of breadsticks and place in a vase for bread flowers.
- Use a golden container to hold bread.

A MORSEL OF BREAD

Display a bread plate as a reminder
of God's presence.

CHAPTER 33

Guarding Bread

*For today in the city of David [Bethlehem] there has been born
for you a Savior, who is Christ the Lord.*

LUKE 2:11

AFTER WORLD WAR II, hundreds of orphans who survived the concentration camps had no home or recollection of their names or families. The British government transported the first three hundred to Windermere, England. The workers noticed that the children had trouble sleeping unless they gave them a slice of bread to hold when they tucked them in. A book that describes the problem is titled, *Sleeping with Bread: Holding What Gives You Life.* The bread provided security, hope, and the faith that they would have food in the morning. The children guarded the bread with their little hands, holding it tightly during the night. At some children's refuge camps during the war, the little ones never had enough bread. They gobbled it quickly and stuffed some in their pockets. Hunger is hard, and bread, even if stale, becomes precious.

One of the children, Minia, recalled seeing homes with gardens for the first time in Windermere. She also remembered being welcomed: "There is this gentleman in the front garden, and he greets me, 'Good morning, what a beautiful day.' And it was a beautiful day—it was wonderful."[1]

The bread gave the children hope and security. Real security and lasting hope come from God. One of the greatest proclamations of hope is found in the message of the angels of the birth of a Savior, born in the House of Bread, the city of David. A day with hope is wonderful.

LOVIN' FROM THE LORD

Then let [the Egyptian workers] gather all the food of these good years that are coming, and store up the grain for food in the cities under Pharaoh's authority, and let them guard it.

GENESIS 41:35

The Old English word for Lord came from *hláford hláf* or *hláfweard*. *Hláf* means "bread or loaf" plus *weard* meaning keeper, guard, or warder and thus a loaf of bread means "bread guarder." Early English Bible translators chose to translate the Latin Vulgate word *dominus* (head of house) into *Lord* when referring to God and Jesus. Thus, in referring to Jesus as Lord, we can also reference Christ as the "bread guarder" or "bread keeper."

From the beginning, God created an intricate plan full of amazing details. *Lord* is used for the term master. Paul referred to the church as one bread, thus connecting Jesus as the guarder of the church. (1 Corinthians 10:17). Protecting the precious grain used for bread goes back to the time of Joseph in Egypt.

> **FOOD FOR THOUGHT**
>
> How does Jesus guard your heart?
>
> What verses give you hope and a sense of security?

The image depicted in the Bible is Jesus as a shepherd guarding His flock of believers. He gave His life for all believers, all members of His church. Psalm 121 is a prayerful reminder that the Lord will guard us. He offers His protection to every believer.

THE JOY OF BREAD MAKING

Store-brand bread names often reflect wholesome nutrition, eating, or words linked to farming, nature, and sunshine. Consider these, for example:

- Healthy Life
- Holsum
- Nature's Pride
- Nature's Harvest
- Country Harvest Stone Milled
- Ezekiel Bread
- Great Value
- Pepperidge Farm (name of plant similar to sour gum)
- Wonder Bread
- Roman Meal
- Earthgrains

Other words, like *rainbow*, allude to being good or connected to God's promise in the rainbow, although they may fall short of providing great nutrition. Associating an item with healthy words makes it attractive. But while grains are good for us, we must look beyond the names to the nutritional facts. The bread label provides important information. Choose breads with:

- 100% whole grain
- Short list of pronounceable ingredients
- Lists of ingredients beginning *whole grain* or *stoneground* and not *enriched flour*
- 120 calories or fewer per slice

- 3 or more grams of fiber per slice
- Sprouted wheat

Avoid products with:

- Refined sugars, especially high fructose corn syrup, which can lead to higher triglycerides and decreased insulin sensitivity (precursor to diabetes)
- Artificial sweeteners
- Trans fat, such as partially hydrogenated oil, which increases bad cholesterol
- Artificial color or flavor
- Potassium bromate, an oxidizing agent, which causes kidney and thyroid tumors in rats
- Azodicarbonamide (ADA), a dough conditioner, which is under investigation as a potential carcinogenic
- Butylated hydroxyanisole (BHA) prevents rancidity, but it is reasonably anticipated by to be a carcinogen from reports by the US Department of Health and Human Services
- Caramel coloring, considered likely by the World Health Organization to be carcinogenic

A MORSEL OF BREAD

Let Jesus be your true wonder bread,
wholesome and filling for your soul.

CHAPTER 34

Sweet Bread

On the first day of the week, when we were gathered together
to break bread, Paul began talking to them, intending to leave
the next day, and he prolonged his message until midnight.

ACTS 20:7

WE LIVED ON A SMALL Coast Guard island when I met Susan, a teen girl in my neighborhood. I asked her to babysit while my husband and I attended Bible study. The first night, I arrived home to a disaster. The children had run circles around her and had emptied every toy and book onto the floor. She was in tears and said she'd understand if I didn't want her to sit again. I gave her a hug, told her to get some rest, and promised we'd talk later. I didn't want to leave things that way; I wanted to prolong my time with her, to help her if I could.

Susan had lost her mother in a tragic accident involving a drunk driver. She had two younger brothers. I helped her learn how to manage the children and coached her to be a good sitter. I also sent her home with fresh bread at times. It turned out her father had a weakness for homemade bread, so even when she was grounded, she could babysit if she'd bring home bread. I taught her to make bread, and we hosted her family for dinner. I served some simple sweet pastry desserts. Soon, Susan had a list of people wanting her to babysit, but she generally asked me if I needed her before committing her time. She also stopped by at times to play with the children or take them to a movie on base.

Sharing our talents is part of fellowship. Jesus poured Himself into the lives of His disciples as He taught them and showed them by example. Consider mentoring a younger person. Share your wisdom, knowledge, and skills, including bread making. Doing so gives them sweet encouragement.

LOVIN' FROM THE LORD

When [Paul] had gone back up and had broken the bread and eaten,
he talked with them a long while until daybreak, and then left.

ACTS 20:11

Paul arrived in Troas at the end of the Feast of Unleavened Bread. He gathered with a group to break bread and talk. He talked so late into the night that one young man fell asleep by a window and fell down three stories to the ground. Men picked him up and noted he had died. Paul stopped preaching, embraced the lad, and told his friends the boy had life in him—he was alive!

At daybreak, Paul broke bread, talked into the morning, and left. The people departed, too, taking the revived young man with them. Paul left the people with the sweet

---

FOOD FOR THOUGHT

What miracles have you experienced?

How do you share the life skills and talents that God has given you?

---

thoughts he had shared and a sweet memory of healing. He also broke bread, a sweet connection with the people that linked them to a special feast around bread as well as Jesus and the Lord's Supper. They may not have had a lot of time together, but they used the time to build memories and learn from Paul's wisdom. God beckons us to share with one another, from our hearts and experience, as well as in fellowship.

LOVIN' FROM THE OVEN

As easily as we can meet someone and build a memory, so we can make a jiffy sweet treat from refrigerator bread. These simple treats are easy to make, using either store-bought refrigerated dough or one of the refrigerated doughs from a recipe in this book.

JIFFY DANISH

Ingredients
    Refrigerated crescent rolls
    Jam or chopped fruits
    Powdered sugar
    Milk

Directions
    Heat oven to 400°F. Open dough and cut into strips. Roll each strip into a long tube or snake. Coil the dough into circles on a lightly greased baking sheet (use a spray or shortening). Plop a teaspoon of filling on the center of each circle.
    Bake 8–10 minutes until lightly browned.
    Mix 1/2 cup powdered sugar with 1 teaspoon of milk (add more milk as needed to make a glaze). Drizzle over pastries.

STUFFED TREATS

Ingredients

Refrigerated crescent rolls

Chocolate chips (milk or white)

Coconut (optional)

Directions

Heat oven to 400°F. Open dough and unroll the triangle shapes. Place a spoonful of chips at wide end. Sprinkle with coconut and roll up. Place on lightly greased baking sheet (use shortening or a cooking spray).

Bake 8–10 minutes until golden brown. If desired, sprinkle with powdered sugar.

A MORSEL OF BREAD

Bread is best enjoyed when shared.

CHAPTER 35

Blended Together

Boaz said to Ruth, "Listen carefully, my daughter.
Do not go to glean in another field; furthermore,
do not go on from this one, but stay here with my maids."
RUTH 2:8

DEVELOPING BONDS WITH new family members is never easy; they don't know the family traditions and activities. Baking bread together has always been a way to encourage new friendships. On my first trip to see my new granddaughters, adopted as teens, we made bread together. The older one enjoyed the process, finding it fascinating and yet sticky. The younger granddaughter loves animals and likes my animal-shaped light wheat bread, especially individual loaves shaped like teddy bears and turtles. Working together in the kitchen is a great way to bond with someone. Now when they visit me, they enjoy homemade breads and especially like fruit breads.

During one visit, we decided to split our dough and make both bread and cinnamon rolls. We rolled out the dough and brushed it with melted butter, sprinkled on cinnamon and sugar, then added raisins on one half and chocolate chips on the other half. Then we rolled it up like a jellyroll and sliced the roll into two-inch thicknesses that we placed in greased pans. Once baked and cooled, we drizzled on glaze and enjoyed eating a few. The next morning, their church fed breakfast to the homeless including the cinnamon rolls and bread we baked. Everyone enjoyed the surprise addition and praised my granddaughters for making the special treat.

We should take advantage of opportunities to share with the younger members of our families and encourage them to be generous. It helps build family bonds. As they understand a healthy family, we hope they will appreciate the family of God and God's call to reach out and help others.

LOVIN' FROM THE LORD

She took it up and went into the city, and her mother-in-law saw what she had gleaned. She also took it out and gave Naomi what she had left after she was satisfied.
RUTH 2:18

Ruth came to Bethlehem as a foreigner. She and her mother-in-law, Naomi, had lived and worked together in the same household in Moab for years. Ruth had observed Naomi and became a believer in the God Naomi followed. She stated she would leave her homeland and go with Naomi They arrived in Bethlehem, both widowed and impoverished. Ruth gleaned in a field for grain for food.

God provided for the poor with laws on gleaning. This meant that harvesters would do a single sweep of reaping and not return to pick up any grain they'd missed. Poor people followed the workers and picked up whatever dropped on the field or was

FOOD FOR THOUGHT

When have you been secretly generous to someone?

How have you mentored someone?

not harvested. It might take a day to gather enough for one meal. Naomi exclaimed at the bounty Ruth had collected. Kernels of grain could be eaten raw or beaten to make flour for bread.

The gleaning brought Ruth into the path of Naomi's rich relative, Boaz. Ruth's dedication to Naomi and hard work led to Boaz noticing her. He admired Ruth's effort and asked about her. He invited Ruth to sit with him at lunch and dipped bread with her. They probably dipped bread in a wine vinegar (sour wine) and, thus, the elements of communion. Unknown to Ruth, Boaz had instructed his men to leave extra for Ruth to glean. His generous spirit reflected God's generosity. Eventually, Ruth and Boaz married, and Ruth gave birth to Obed, the grandfather of King David. God blessed the meeting that started in a grain field.

LOVIN' FROM THE OVEN

This is a light wheat bread that uses both white and whole wheat flour. Make it in the shape of a guest's favorite animal. Shaping bread reminds me how Jesus shapes our lives, often in unexpected ways, and reshapes our families with new members.

LIGHT WHEAT TEDDY BEAR BREAD

Ingredients

1 cup wheat flour	1/2 cup warm milk
2 cups white flour, divided	1 tablespoon butter
1 package active dry yeast	1/2 cup water
1 tablespoon sugar	1 egg, beaten
1 teaspoon salt	

Directions

Mix 1 cup wheat flour, 1/2 cup white flour, yeast, sugar, and salt in a bowl.

Heat milk to hot but not boiling. Add butter and stir until melted.

Stir milk, butter, and water into flour mixture. Add egg and stir. Stir in enough of remaining flour to make dough that is firm but not too stiff.

Sprinkle flour on surface and place dough onto flour. Knead until smooth and elastic (about 5 minutes). Cover dough and let rise 10 minutes.

Pull off sections of dough and shape to form animals, such as a teddy bear. Make several small ones or one large. Cover and let rise 25–30 minutes.

Heat oven to 400°F.

Teddy Bear Shaping

Shape and place bread on greased baking sheet. Roll a large ball for belly, a smaller ball for head, and small balls for ears and paws. Place the smaller balls of dough slightly under the main body or head and press together. Press in raisins for eyes or roll tiny balls of dough.

Bake until the top turns golden brown, 25–30 minutes (decrease time if you make smaller animals); if needed, cover loosely with foil after ten minutes of baking to prevent crust from getting too dark.

Turtle Shaping

Make a large round ball for turtle shell, add a head, four feet, and a thin tail. Use a knife to make a pattern on shell. Add raisin eyes.

Bake as for the bear-shaped bread.

MORSEL OF BREAD

Working together in a kitchen builds bonds and provides opportunity to mentor others.

Steps in Bread Making

Bread making is truly one of the great dramas in the kitchen. Simple ingredients transform through mixing, beating, punching down, and kneading to form bread. Each step of making a yeast bread reflects a step in our own journey to becoming more like Christ, the Bread of Life.

CHAPTER 36

Gather and Measure Ingredients

Thus You grow grain for bread, grapes for wine, grass for cattle—
all of this for us. And so we have bread to make our bodies strong,
wine to make our hearts happy, oil to make our faces shine.
Every good thing we need, Your earth provides;
our faces grow flush with Your life in them.

Psalm 104:14–15 voice

MY COUSIN CATHY AND I always enjoyed Thanksgiving Eve at our Grandma Doody's home. We stayed up late preparing the food for the next day's feast. We piled all ingredients high on one counter. The house smelled of pumpkin, apples, sage, parsley, cranberries, cinnamon, and other fall aromas. We baked breads, dressed the turkey, ground ingredients for relishes, whipped cream to go with pies, and always tried new recipes. We laughed and talked the night away as we kept busy in the small kitchen.

One year, Grandma found a recipe for cranberry- and apple-filled candy cane pastries. Cathy chopped apples and added cinnamon and sugar while I chopped cranberries and added orange peel and raisins. Grandma prepared the yeast dough. We divided the dough and each spooned on the fillings we had made. We folded the filled dough into three layers and sliced it into strips. We twisted the strips and shaped them into canes before placing them on greased baking sheets. After baking and cooling, we added a glaze, tinting one red for the apple-filled pastry canes.

That day, our extended family gathered for the feast followed by card games. We expressed thanks for our many blessings and talked about the first Thanksgiving and God's provision of friends and food. Community thanksgiving and feasting brings a sense of belonging and shared praise for God's blessings.

FOOD FOR THOUGHT

Do people recognize that you are a Christian?

How have you become more like Jesus?

LOVIN' FROM THE LORD

His winnowing fork is in His hand, and He will thoroughly clear His threshing floor; and He will gather His wheat into the barn, but He will burn up the chaff with unquenchable fire.

MATTHEW 3:12

There are several steps in making yeast breads, and much more that happens to grow seed and turn it into flour. Jesus, the Bread of Life, is also a bread maker.

He invites each of us to follow His example and become like Him. He wants to transform each of us into Christians who will make a difference in this world. Jesus, the bread maker, works with us in our lives, to make us like Him.

John the Baptist described Jesus coming and winnowing, threshing, gathering the good wheat, and burning the chaff. This prophesied about Jesus separating His followers from the unbelievers. Jesus compared the believers who followed Him to good wheat.

The first step in making bread is gathering the ingredients. God begins changing us as we gather near Him. He has all the ingredients needed—gifts of the Holy Spirit, character-building opportunities, and wisdom. He is the skillful baker who transforms us from our raw forms to more Christlike followers.

Christians are described in 2 Corinthians 2:14–15 as a fragrance of Christ to God. How much sweeter we should be than a Thanksgiving feast. We're an aroma of life!

LOVIN' FROM THE OVEN

As a child I remember my family looked forward to Christmas starting on Thanksgiving. That included a tradition of making these Christmas cane pastries for our November holiday. The time between the holidays can be exciting and filled with advent activities that help families focus on the coming of Christ. Make these sweet pastry canes to enjoy as you think about waiting for special times. Leave them as sticks instead of canes to enjoy any time of year.

CHRISTMAS PASTRY CANES

Dough Ingredients

1/4 cup lukewarm water	1 teaspoon grated lemon peel
1 package active dry yeast	2 eggs
1 cup milk	1 cup margarine
3/4 cup sugar	Red and white frosting (using
4 cups flour	canned or your favorite
1 teaspoon salt	recipe)

Directions

Dissolve yeast in warm water for ten minutes.

Scald milk, then cool to lukewarm and set aside. Combine sugar, flour, salt, and lemon peel in a bowl. Add milk and yeast mix to bowl and mix. Cover dough tightly and refrigerate 2 hours.

Heat oven to 400°F. Divide dough in half and roll each half into 18x5-inch rectangle.

Spread 1 filling on each rectangle. Fold dough in 3 layers for a 6x15-inch rectangle. Cut each into 15 strips. Twist each strip and shape into a candy cane while placing on a greased baking sheet.

Bake 10–15 minutes until bottoms are golden brown.

Cool and frost. Use red frosting on apple canes and white on cranberry canes.

CRANBERRY FILLING

Ingredients

1 1/2 cups chopped cranberries	1/2 cup raisins
1/2 cup sugar	1/3 cup honey
1/3 cup nuts (pecans or almonds)	1 1/2 teaspoons orange peel

Directions

Combine all ingredients and cook over medium heat 5 minutes; cool before filling pastry.

APPLE FILLING

Ingredients

1 1/2 cups chopped, peeled, apples	1/3 cup sugar
3/4 cup pecans, chopped	1 tablespoon cinnamon

Directions

Combine all ingredients and cook over medium heat 5 minutes; cool before filling pastry.

A MORSEL OF BREAD

Remember that Jesus gathers us
together in His presence
to shape us into one bread.

CHAPTER 37

Dissolved

With the sacrifice of his peace offerings
for thanksgiving, he shall present his offering
with cakes of leavened bread.

LEVITICUS 7:13

MY HEART BROKE for my friend and her family. They had just received news that shattered their hearts. The police had arrested their son for a terrible crime, and I cried for her. I thawed a loaf of bread from the freezer and drove to her home. I gave them my little offering and sat with them. They poured out their hearts as I listened and felt some of their pain. As I left, they expressed thanks and said that God had been reminding them of Scriptures, and our talk had brought them some peace.

I've given bread to many people, including to friends after we've had a disagreement. It's an offering of peace and something sweet to ease the pain in someone's heart. As I make bread, I pray for those who will eat it. I pray for peace and blessings in their lives. I start praying as I open the yeast to dissolve it.

In biblical times and in early colonial days, women used a little leavened dough from a previous batch to mix into the flour while making dough. This spread the leaven, or yeast, throughout and produced what we call sourdough. Other yeast breads are started by dissolving yeast in warm water.

Yeast is a living organism that, without water, remains dormant, dry, and useless. Water separates the cells of the yeast, softening them so they open and grow.

Our hearts also need water to revive them. Jesus provides water in our hearts, and it often mixes with tears of sorrow, frustration, or hurt until the rough emotions dissolve with love.

LOVIN' FROM THE LORD

Now on the last day, the great day of the feast,
Jesus stood and cried out, saying,
"If anyone is thirsty, let him come to Me and drink."
JOHN 7:37

Jesus calls anyone who thirsts to come to Him. When we do, God begins transforming us to be like Jesus. We come to Him and are baptized with water. His waters and His love fill our inner beings—our souls and hearts. Our troubles dissolve in time when we place our problems with Jesus.

Jesus called out these words of comfort and encouragement on the last day of a special feast, called the Feast of Tabernacles, Feast of Booths, or Sukkot. On the seventh

> **FOOD FOR THOUGHT**
>
> How does Jesus quench your thirst?
>
> When have you been parched and thankful for water?

day of this festival, the priests led a procession and poured water around the altar seven times. That illustrates the joy associated with water.

The feast follows Yom Kippur, the Day of Atonement. The entire fall season of feasts begins with Rosh Hashanah, the New Year. Jesus's words were delivered at a time of asking God for forgiveness. We start our walk with Jesus when we come and ask for forgiveness. He cleanses us with baptism. It is a time of newness as a person becomes a Christian. It's time for Him to give us the living waters of the Holy Spirit.

The past is dissolved and new growth begins with water.

LOVIN' FROM THE OVEN

Some breads are moist and filled with flavor. When I first tried this bread made by a new Hispanic friend, I asked for the recipe. She wrote it out in her broken English and drew a few sketches to hope I would understand. When we like a homemade food, we want more and often ask for the recipe. That's what can happen when we first get a taste of the Christian life. We want more; we want Jesus.

This recipe comes from someone who seldom measured her ingredients, so it has a wide range of flour and water. We bridged our different cultures and languages with bread. I found I needed less water. The dough was very sticky when I turned it out to knead the first time, and I added more flour until it was firm but still very soft. The amount of flour and water varies more by altitude. I live at sea level, so I need less liquid and more flour. I've helped friends figure out recipes from their grandmothers and other family members that use terms like handfuls of flour. The key is generally the description of the dough (soft or stiff). As you make more breads, you learn how the dough feels.

JOSEFA'S ORANGE BREAD

Ingredients

2 packages active dry yeast

1/2 cup warm water

1/2 cup butter

1/4 cup shortening

1/2 to 1 cup sugar

1 teaspoon salt

2 large eggs

2 tablespoons grated orange

   zest from 1 fresh orange

1/2 cup orange juice (squeeze

   from same orange)

2–3 cups warm water

6–9 cups unbleached flour

1 cup raisins

Directions

Dissolve yeast with warm water in small bowl for ten minutes.

In large bowl, cream together butter, shortening, sugar, salt, and eggs (add eggs 1 at a time). Add orange zest and juice and beat well. Stir in yeast mixture. Add 1 cup warm water and stir. Add 2 cups of flour. Add raisins. Add more water as needed to make soft but firm dough. *(The amount of flour needed varies with humidity in the air. If it starts to be hard to mix, it is getting too firm. Add a few tablespoons of water to soften it again.)*

Knead for a few minutes, adding flour as needed so dough is not sticky but remains soft. Place in greased bowl. Turn dough to grease all sides. Let rise 2–3 hours, till doubled.

Knead and braid bread, form rolls, or divide dough into 2 or 3, 9x5 inch bread pans. Let rise again, about 1–2 hours.

Bake at 350°F for 1 hour (30–40 minutes for rolls) until golden.

A MORSEL OF BREAD

When you dissolve in tears,
trust that God is using that time
to raise you up with new hope.

CHAPTER 38

Making a Smooth Batter

*Grain for bread is crushed, indeed, he does not continue
to thresh it forever. Because the wheel of his cart and his horses
eventually damage it, he does not thresh it longer*

Isaiah 28:28

THE KERNEL OF WHEAT is separated from the chaff by beating or grinding. For yeast breads, the dough is kneaded and patted to make it smooth and elastic. How we treat the wheat and the dough changes the outcomes we desire.

How we treat children makes a difference, too, as we mold them through example, lessons, and guidance. And people will notice the outcome. Intent as a pirate digging for buried treasure, a distressed mother probed my mind, seeking gems of wisdom. Her child's latest escapades had led her to seek my counsel. It made me wonder, "Do I wear a sign: mother who miraculously converted five unruly, manner-challenged heathens into socially acceptable adults who love the Lord—call for treasure map and complete directions!" Our parenting path would more resemble a family circus than a treasure hunt!

Our oldest son's school called often with news of his latest escapades. Our older daughter reacted to teasing and tiffs with lamenting she was destined to never have a real friend in the world. Our younger daughter found it difficult to be in a lower grade than her very bright brothers where teachers expected her to perform like they did. Each child brought unique challenges. As in stirring batter rapidly, we needed to respond quickly to our children. We made rules, sometimes on the fly, with appropriate consequences. We worked to stir their hearts, adding in faith to raise adults with great character.

My children's cries of unfair treatment echo my response to God's discipline. Through raising children, I realized God's loving care made me a better person, just as stirring batter creates better bread.

LOVIN' FROM THE LORD

His winnowing fork is in His hand, and He will thoroughly clear
His threshing floor; and He will gather His wheat into the barn,
but He will burn up the chaff with unquenchable fire.

MATTHEW 3:12

Beating the wheat, or threshing it, loosens the grain from the stalk and husk. It falls onto the threshing floor. The next step is winnowing. It's normally done in an open space, often on a hill, where the wind can blow away the lighter chaff when the farmer tosses the grain into the air. The wheat is stored, but the useless chaff is blown away.

God used the image of threshing in the Old Testament as a symbol of disciplining His people as described

FOOD FOR THOUGHT

How has God separated out sin in your life?

How is God disciplining you now?

in a king who winnows the wicked and drives a threshing wheel over them (Proverbs 20:26).

Jesus described the end times as a time when wheat is gathered while the chaff is burned. God wants to gather His followers together for a joyful crowd of believers. That helps us see the peacefulness and fruitfulness in heaven.

God disciplines those he loves (Hebrews 12:7, 11) to promote fruitful growth He separates out our sin and selfishness and brings out truth and strengthens us. He wants wants His discipline to yield the fruit of peace.

LOVIN' FROM THE OVEN

My grandmother made great rolls for sandwiches. She made them from scratch for years until she found a mix that worked as well as her own recipe. Sometimes there is nothing better than a great shortcut, especially when you get the same results with half the work.

GRANDMA'S FLUFFY SANDWICH ROLLS

Ingredients

1 16-ounce package hot roll mix (or use 3 1/3 cups of DIY mix following directions below)

1 package active dry yeast
1 cup hot water (120–130°F)
2 tablespoons butter, softened
1 egg

Directions

Heat oven to 350°F. Grease 13x9-inch baking pan. Combine hot roll mix and yeast in bowl; mix well. Add hot water, butter, and egg; stir until soft dough forms. Turn dough out onto lightly floured surface; knead dough 5 minutes until smooth. Cover dough with bowl and let rest 5 minutes.

Divide dough into 12 equal pieces and roll to 1-inch thick circles for sandwich rolls. Place in pan, cover, and let rise in warm place for 30 minutes or until doubled in size. Bake for 16–18 minutes or until golden brown.

Brush tops of warm rolls with 2 tablespoons melted butter, if desired.

To prepare ahead

Make as above but stop before baking; cover loosely with plastic wrap. Chill up to 24 hours in refrigerator.

When ready to bake, let stand at room temperature until doubled in size. Bake at 350°F for 30 minutes.

DIY MIX FOR HOT ROLLS

Ingredients

10 cups flour

3/4 cup nonfat dry milk
  powder

3/4 cup sugar

4 teaspoons salt

3/4 cup butter-flavored
  shortening

Directions

In large bowl, mix flour, powdered milk, sugar, and salt. Cut in shortening until crumbly or mix in food processor. Store in airtight container until ready to use.

Makes 4 batches.

A MORSEL OF BREAD

When you feel beaten down,
trust that God is working.

CHAPTER 39

Waiting for the Dough to Rise

So then, my brethren, when you come together to eat,
wait for one another.

1 Corinthians 11:33

IN PREPARING FOR FRANK, the local television station's camera operator, to film me making bread and cinnamon rolls, I prepared three batches of dough. That would work around all the rising times.

I mixed my first batch early and punched the dough down thirty minutes before Frank arrived. I mixed the second batch ninety minutes before Frank arrived.

I shaped two loaves from the first batch and placed them in the oven just before his arrival. I formed cinnamon rolls from the remaining dough of that batch. Frank arrived and set up while I placed the rolls in the oven. He taped my removing the bread and rolls from the oven and punching down the second batch of dough. While the second batch rested, Frank filmed me discussing ingredients and bread-making tips.

Making three batches at different intervals helped Frank film all the steps in a single hour: mixing, kneading, shaping dough into loaves, and baking. He recorded me rolling out dough for cinnamon rolls, covering it with butter, cinnamon, sugar, and raisins, rolling it up, slicing it, and placing buns in greased pans. He also filmed as I made the glaze and drizzled it over the cooled cinnamon rolls. When we finished taping, Frank left with fresh bread for communion at his church and cinnamon rolls for the station's crew. I later finished the last batch when it finished rising.

FOOD FOR THOUGHT

What helps you relax and rest?

What are you waiting on now?

Waiting is part of life. Change, including our inner character growth, takes time. And God allows us to wait on answers because He knows the perfect timing.

Paul spoke about waiting for all to arrive before breaking bread. He wanted people to celebrate as a group. It's a reminder that we should be patient with other people as they grow and change.

LOVIN' FROM THE LORD

This was done on the thirteenth day of the month Adar,
and on the fourteenth day they rested
and made it a day of feasting and rejoicing.
ESTHER 9:17

In the days of Esther, when God delivered His people, they rested and feasted. This happened after a time they had been stirred up with fear and then delivered. The time of resting also gave them time to rise up and celebrate God's protection.

Dough must be covered and allowed to sit in a warm place to rise. Rising takes time and warmth. We are covered or protected by God our Father and kept in the warmth of His love. We wait upon the Lord's timing. He allows us to rest and grow as we trust Him.

Some bread recipes call for a second rising. This is usually a shorter time than the first and is done to make the dough hold its shape. Likewise, on occasion we need to continue waiting in life. We learn to endure. James 1:4 teaches, "Let endurance have its perfect result, so that you may be perfect and complete, lacking in nothing." Just as a good baker knows the importance of timing in the dough, so God, our Creator, knows perfect timing in our lives.

I have waited for my children's births, for my husband's return from deployments at sea, for editors to respond to writing submissions, for houses to sell, and more. Each time, the waiting was worth it.

Resting is good for people too. It is often in the resting that we rise.

LOVIN' FROM THE OVEN

In filming the bread making, we realized we couldn't capture the aroma. Sharing how to make the sweet rolls is the next best thing.

It's great that bread dough is so adaptable. The first time I used my wheat dough for cinnamon buns, it was a hit. Follow the recipe for Honey-of-an-Egg Whole Wheat Bread (page 33) to make the dough. Use the dough for one loaf of bread to make one pan of rolls. The dough is rolled out, covered with the filling, rolled up like a jellyroll, sliced, baked, and then topped with a glaze. Frozen dough from the store can also be thawed and used.

BREAKFAST CINNAMON ROLLS

Ingredients

Whole wheat bread dough (page 33) or other dough for one loaf of bread

1/4 cup butter, melted

1/2 cup sugar

2 tablespoons cinnamon

1 cup raisins, cranraisins, chocolate chips, or nuts as desired

1/2 cup powdered sugar

1/2 teaspoon vanilla

2–3 tablespoons milk

Directions

Heat oven to 350°F. Roll out the dough into a 14x12-inch rectangle. Brush with melted butter. Combine the sugar and cinnamon, then sprinkle mix over dough. Sprinkle on raisins or other filling.

Roll up jellyroll style. Slice every two inches, turn up so the filling shows, and place on greased baking sheet or in a greased 9x13-inch pan. Cover with a dry, clean kitchen towel and let rise 20 minutes.

Bake for 20–30 minutes, until lightly brown and cooked through.

Let cool. Combine powdered sugar, vanilla, and milk to form glaze; drizzle over rolls.

A MORSEL OF BREAD

In times of waiting,
enjoy a bite of bread and thank God
that everything is in His hands.

CHAPTER 40

Whack! The Necessary Punch

*The LORD is near to the brokenhearted
and saves those who are crushed in spirit.*

PSALM 34:18

THE WORDS STUNNED ME: "Mom had a stroke. She may not recover." The next morning, doctors rushed Mom into the operating room because she had had a cerebral hemorrhage.

My mother came through the surgery, and then, while receiving blood thinners, started having blood clots in her legs. In reversing meds, she suffered a second cerebral hemorrhage. She took eighteen months to recover, but she eventually walked again and never lost her speech or mental processing. She lived many more years.

That news, and years later the news that my husband had stage four breast cancer, were hard blows. Each time, I felt like I had been punched and could hardly breathe. Yet we rose above the problems and used them to encourage others.

My husband received the news that he had two to three months to live, but God graciously gave us two and a half more years together, with good health most of that time.

Over the years, I've faced many other blows, some that crushed my spirit. Crushed is another term used with grain; crushing turns the kernels into flour. We can rise above the punches we receive in life when we give thanks for the blessings and trust God through the pain. We can be thankful for the years and great memories.

God helps change us as He allows us to be crushed and helps us be more usable. For me, trials and hardships produced endurance and a deeper appreciation of my health and the family and friends who love me. I grew stronger and my compassion increased. I grew closer to my children. God used those times to transform my heart and character.

LOVIN' FROM THE LORD

The field is ruined, the land mourns; for the grain is ruined,
the new wine dries up, fresh oil fails.
JOEL 1:10

The threshing floors will be full of grain,
and the vats will overflow with the new wine and oil.
JOEL 2:24

When the dough finishes rising, we are told to punch it down in the center. We watch it deflate and listen as air escapes. In the oven, surrounded by warmed air, it will rise again and bake to perfection.

Dough does not always rise in the suggested time. The test that dough has finished rising is not only that it has doubled in size but also how it responds to another test. Take a spoon or grease your finger and gently push it into the dough about an inch. If the dough does not puff back up and the dent remains, it is ready. Richer dough with sugar, eggs, and fat ingredients takes longer to rise. Dough made at lower altitudes also takes longer to rise.

Without the hard punch, the dough would never become the airy, delicious bread we love to eat. Without hard knocks in life, we might never become the strong individuals God created us to be. The prophets reminded the people that if they followed idols, God would send punishment. Joel prophesied that a hard-hitting punch of crop failure would cause famine and hardship. But God also promised that when they turned back, He would restore them and bless them abundantly. God used those times to turn people's hearts back to Himself. We don't always know the reasons for our problems except that we live in a fallen world, but we can place our eternal hope in God.

> **FOOD FOR THOUGHT**
>
> Have you ever felt like you were being punched down?
>
> When have you become more usable after a crushing experience?

James 1:2–3 reminds us to have a godly, different perspective, "Consider it all joy, my brethren, when you encounter various trials, knowing that the testing of your faith produces endurance." Trust God to fill the emptiness of being punched in.

LOVIN' FROM THE OVEN

Breads can become edible containers to hold other foods, like these muffins with a sloppy joe filling. They are like little individual meat pies.

MEAL IN A MUFFIN

Ingredients

Biscuit dough (homemade
or 2 packages refrigerated
biscuits)
1 pound ground beef
2 tablespoons chopped
scallions

2/3 cup barbecue sauce
2 tablespoons brown sugar
1 cup shredded or sliced
cheddar or mozzarella cheese

Directions

Heat oven to 400°F. Use one biscuit rolled into a 2-inch balls. Press each ball of dough into a greased muffin tin (use shortening).

Cook ground beef and scallions. Add barbecue sauce and brown sugar to beef. Spoon beef filling into muffin cups. Place cheese on top (grated or sliced).

Bake for 8–10 minutes, until cooked through and edge of muffins are golden.

Makes 20

A MORSEL OF BREAD

Life may throw hard punches,
but that allows God to make a better you.

CHAPTER 41

Kneading

*She rises also while it is still night and gives food
to her household and portions to her maidens.*

PROVERBS 31:15

MY FRIEND, PEGGY SUE WELLS, shared this story, describing herself
as the "practical Marilla Cuthbert" while her four-year-old middle child,
Leilani, resembled the "artistic Anne of Green Gables." Leilani learned differently, processed differently, and saw beauty in places Peggy Sue hadn't
even noticed were places.

When Peggy Sue prayed for wisdom to understand Leilani and her
unique gifts, God impressed on Peggy Sue to give her the gift of music.
She telephoned Mary Ann, the only local piano teacher. Mary Ann's
schedule was full, but she added Peggy Sue to her years-long waiting list.

Surprisingly, Mary Ann called back a few days later.

"I've been praying about this," she said. "I can squeeze in a half-hour
each week. I feel strongly that I should use it to teach your middle child."

Mary Ann appreciated Leilani's qualities and helped Peggy Sue embrace her daughter's unique personality. Often after lessons, Mary Ann invited them for tea. While the children played, Mary Ann served delicious scones with flaky crusts, airy centers, and dark chocolate chips. The delicious clouds of comfort became a family favorite.

One day, Leilani practiced while Peggy Sue took a turn making scones.

"Mama, was Bach a nice man?" Leilani asked.

"I believe so," Peggy Sue answered. "He wrote those minuets to teach his wife and children how to play piano."

"Good. Then he won't mind that I am fixing his music," she said.

Leilani played her original rendition for Mary Ann, who applauded the creative arrangement. She then modeled a teaching technique as she asked Leilani to play the score once to hear how Bach composed it.

Mary Ann became cheerleader, coauthor, confidante, and prayer mentor. As Anne of Green Gables would say, Mary Ann became bosom friend to both Leilani and Peggy Sue. It's good to have and become a prayerful mentor.

LOVIN' FROM THE LORD

She looks well to the ways of her household,
and does not eat the bread of idleness.
PROVERBS 31:27

The word *lady* comes from an Old English word meaning "kneader of bread" or "loaf-kneader." A lady would know the right time to give the loaf a push! This excellent wife rose early to feed her family. A woman had to rise early to allow time for making bread.

We think of a lady as a woman who is refined and polite with gracious manners, like Mary Ann. She also uses her time wisely. In 2 John 1:1–6, John beckons a lady to practice something that will make her refined in a godly way. More than mere hospitality and filling stomachs, God wants us to love others.

We move from satisfying a person's need for survival to fellowship when we love generously. That includes spending portions of our time with those in need.

God wants bread to be a reminder of generosity and helping others. We should barely say the words "Give us this day our daily bread" without thinking about feeding hungry hearts and souls. I've never been an early riser like the woman in Proverbs 31, but I've always intentionally focused on hospitality and blessing others. Use your talents generously to mentor and friend someone else. That's the mark of a real lady.

> **FOOD FOR THOUGHT**
>
> When and how have you been refined?
>
> Kneading makes bread more elastic. What helps you be more elastic in life?

LOVIN' FROM THE OVEN

A scone is an individual quick bread that is only lightly sweetened and often served with other sweeteners like honey, jam, or cream. It's a favorite treat with tea in the British Isles. This recipe comes from Mary Ann, who is from Scotland. Peggy Sue says, when she first made these, everyone devoured them quickly and remarked on how they were so light and tasty. The recipe is now part of Peggy Sue's family celebrations and gatherings. You may want to add it to your favorites too.

MARY ANN'S CHOCOLATE CHIP SCONES

Ingredients

1 cup butter

1/4 cup plus 2 tablespoons sugar

3 eggs

1/3 cup buttermilk or yogurt

3 cups flour

1 tablespoon baking powder

1/2 cup chocolate chips

Directions

Beat butter on high until creamy. Add sugar, beat 5 minutes till fluffy. Add eggs one at a time; stir and add flour and baking powder, blending thoroughly. Add buttermilk or yogurt and mix only until blended. Fold in chocolate chips; if desired, add other ingredients including pecans, orange rind, etc.

Divide dough into thirds and roll into circles; prick each circle into pie wedges to make cutting after baking easier; cover with plastic wrap and refrigerate 45 minutes (this gives the scones that crunchy top) or freeze and when hard place in a plastic bag for baking later.

Heat oven to 350°F and bake each circle for 15 minutes. Decrease heat to 325°F and continue baking for 13 minutes until golden.

SWEET WHIPPED CREAM

Ingredients

1 cup heavy whipping cream, cold

Powdered sugar (about 3–4 tablespoons)

Flavoring if desired (vanilla or one that matches jam or scone being served)

Directions

Beat cream on medium speed. Increase to high speed and beat until thick, fluffy, soft peaks form. Gradually add powdered sugar, one tablespoon at a time, until desired sweetness. If desired, add 1 teaspoon vanilla or other flavoring.

A MORSEL OF BREAD

As kneading makes the dough elastic,
so God makes you more flexible.

CHAPTER 42

Shaping the Bread

For the bread of God is that which comes down out of heaven,
and gives life to the world.

JOHN 6:33

"TRY THE BREAD. IT'S GOOD. You'll want to buy some," I yelled.

Our church in Miami recreated the scene of the town of Bethlehem, including merchant stalls, an inn, and a stable with Jesus. Visitors arrived first to Herod's palace and then traveled on to Bethlehem.

Actors performed as shepherds, merchants, rabbis, and others to give an authentic setting of the first Christmas. I performed the part of a baker. An outdoor oven with an opening in the back had hot charcoal and heated stones that made it possible to cook bread. I premade dough, and my assistant bakers rolled the dough into small balls, flattened, and shaped them into tiny cakes. We baked them on small cookie trays.

We made the oven from a thick cardboard box. We cut three sides to form a hinged door. We covered the box with heavy-duty foil, inside and out. We added an oven rack made from heavy wire, about one-third from the bottom. A pan held the charcoal and stones.

Shepherd actors cooked lamb over a small fire pit. The choir sang Christmas hymns as visitors waited in line to enter. Visitors became part of the people being counted. They enjoyed the sights, sounds, and aromas. They then walked around a corner to a cave lit by a torch. They saw live animals and real parents with their baby acting as the holy family. Visitors stood in silence as they gazed at the scene, reflecting on the birth of Christ.

LOVIN' FROM THE LORD

Solomon also made all the things that were in the house of God: even the golden altar, the tables with the bread of the Presence on them.
2 CHRONICLES 4:19

God gave specific directions on how to fashion the table to hold the bread of the Presence. God had directed His people to follow His plans for every part of the altar and items in the tabernacle. Made by hand and shaped according to the plan, every detail mattered. God cared about the shape of the loaves and the table on which the priests placed the bread. He cares about details, like the first place where Jesus would rest.

A feeding trough seems an unlikely contrast to a golden table, but it reflected the future of Jesus as the sacrificial Lamb, and it became a temporary table for the Bread of Life. Christ became man. Shepherds arrived, the first visitors to see the Savior. Later, wise men from the east arrived and saw Jesus. Each child born is shaped in the womb by God, carefully formed

---

FOOD FOR THOUGHT

What are some of your favorite memories of celebrating the meaning of Christmas?

How is God molding and changing you?

---

and transformed from a few cells into an intricate person, made to become more like Jesus, the Bread of Life.

There are many ways to shape bread. We can scoop batter into a pan and let the pan's shape form the bread's shape. We can shape dough by hand and form loaves. Dough can be rolled, cut in strips, and braided. It can also be molded by twisting and pressing it to the desired shape.

God molds each of us. He is the potter and we are the dough, or clay, as depicted in Jeremiah 18:6.

LOVIN' FROM THE OVEN

I grew up in New England where cranberries grew in a nearby state, and we used them during the holidays. Years later, I lived in Hawaii and discovered the joy of cooking with macadamia nuts. Now I live in Florida, with luscious oranges.

I've married those flavors with bread that reflects places I've lived and worshiped by changing a recipe given to me by my friend, Sarah Weinstein, a resident of Massachusetts, home of the cranberry bog.

HOLIDAY MACADAMIA NUT
CRANBERRY BREAD

Ingredients

2 cups flour	1 tablespoon grated orange peel
1 cup sugar	2 tablespoon shortening
1 1/2 teaspoons baking powder	1 egg
1 teaspoon salt	1 cup chopped or halved
1/2 teaspoon baking soda	cranberries
3/4 cup orange juice	1 cup chopped macadamia nuts

Directions

Heat oven to 350°F. In a large mixing bowl, combine flour, sugar, baking powder, salt, and soda. Stir to mix well. Add orange juice and peel, shortening, and eggs to dry ingredients. Mix until well blended. Stir in cranberries and chopped nuts.

Turn into a 9x5-inch loaf pan that has been greased on bottom only. Bake for 55–65 minutes, until it browns on top and toothpick inserted in center comes. Cool thoroughly before slicing.

Helpful hints

- Triple the recipe for a hungry crowd
- It's great made with blueberries or blackberries. The dark berries makes the bread a very becoming purple color.
- Try nuts from your region of the country.

A MORSEL OF BREAD

God is the baker who shapes us.

CHAPTER 43

Baking to Perfection

It shall be prepared with oil on a griddle. When it is well stirred,
you shall bring it. You shall present the grain offering
in baked pieces as a soothing aroma to the LORD.

LEVITICUS 6:21

BEN FRANKLIN DESCRIBED HIMSELF upon arrival to Philadelphia as being hungry with little money and a desire for bread. He met a boy with a basket of bread who directed him to a bakery:

> I asked for biscuits, meaning such as we had in Boston; that sort it seems, was not made in Philadelphia. I then asked for a three-penny loaf, and was told they had none. Not knowing the different prices, nor the names of the different sorts of bread, I told him to give me threepenny worth of any sort. He gave me accordingly three great puffy rolls. I was surprised by the quantity, but took it, and, having no room in my pockets, walked off with a roll under each arm, and eating the other.[1]

One roll baked to perfection filled him; he saw a woman and her young son and gave the other rolls to them. He shared his bounty.

In colonial days, town bakeries sprung up that baked distinct breads, often reflecting the nationalities of the settlers. Travelers could often find the bakery by following the scent of fresh bread. Colonists knew the hardships of forging a country and developed a spirit of generosity, helping one another. Passing on the bounty of the rolls was a common gesture of goodwill. Ben Franklin found his new home to be a friendly place and did his part to make the city as welcoming as the aroma of its unique, fresh bread.

LOVIN' FROM THE LORD

Thanks be to God, who always leads us in His triumph in Christ,
and manifests through us the sweet aroma
of the knowledge of Him in every place.

2 CORINTHIANS 2:14

God is transforming us within our hearts. As we grow in our faith and follow Christ we will develop an aroma of Christ that others will notice.

Scents trigger memories and can become associated with people or experiences. In Israel, the aroma of the grain offering, as the person preparing the offering stirred the grain in the oil on a griddle, or baked it in an oven, the aroma would have filled the air. We know the scent of food cooking carries far. People understood the connection of the knowledge of God to a sweet aroma.

A gift of fresh bread with a pleasing aroma and a note with a prayer or a Scripture can also connect others to you through specific

FOOD FOR THOUGHT

How has God's timing worked in your life?

What is God letting bake to perfection in you now?

memories, reminding them of your faith and perhaps inspiring them to talk to you when they have questions about God.

Bread takes time to make and bake to perfection. It also takes time for God to mold us and prepare us for the work He wants us to do. Jesus told His disciples to wait until the Spirit came upon them. They did that, and their witness changed the world.

LOVIN' FROM THE OVEN

The secrets to making popovers are to have a light touch in mixing (do not overmix) and to use a very hot oven. I love the ease and simplicity of them. Settlers from Maine Americanized Yorkshire pudding by creating popovers. Today, they are a reminder of the variety of breads available, even in colonial days.

POPOVERS

Ingredients
>   2 large eggs
>   1 cup milk
>   3 tablespoons melted butter, divided
>   1 cup flour
>   1/4 teaspoon salt

Directions

Heat oven to 450°F. Place muffin or popover tin in oven to heat for a few minutes before adding batter. With a whisk, beat eggs slightly, then blend in milk and 1 tablespoon melted butter. Add flour and salt and beat just until smooth.

Remove pan from oven and butter the cups with the remaining 2 tablespoons melted butter. Whip the batter one more time and then pour into 6 muffin cups, filling each half full.

Bake 15 minutes (**Do not** open door during this part of baking or popovers will deflate). Reduce heat to 350°F and bake another 15 minutes.

Check popovers for doneness: they should look golden brown, feel dry to the touch, and sound hollow when tapped lightly. When done, remove from oven. Remove popovers from pan, turning them upside down on a cooling rack. Prick the bottoms to let steam escape; be careful as the steam can burn skin. Serve while hot.

For a dessert, serve with honey or whipped cream.

A MORSEL OF BREAD

Bread making is an art form
where we indulge in the result
with enthusiasm.

Conditions of Bread

We can buy fresh bread and forget to enjoy it. We let the bread get stale, crumble, mold, or harden. Those conditions mirror what we let happen to our hearts and lives when we neglect God.

God provides for us, but we sometimes ignore God's provision. In learning how to care for bread and how to enjoy it, we can discover how to better nurture our relationship with the Lord.

CHAPTER 44

Moldy Bread

But they did not listen to Moses, and some left part of it
until morning, and it bred worms and became foul;
and Moses was angry with them.

Exodus 16:20

AFTER FEEDING MY FIVE CHILDREN and their assorted friends, I searched for leftovers to eat. I spotted a few slices of bread, but to my dismay, I discovered mold growing on them! "Alas," I thought, "Lord, does this reflect my life? Do I neglect things instead of using them? Do I forget to take preventive measures, like properly storing bread?"

Lightning struck our home in Connecticut twice. Another adventure came when the fuse box went up in flames, engulfing one level of the house with smoke damage. Adding to these adventures in living, Hurricane Gloria barreled down our street, relandscaped our yard, and left us without power for more than two weeks.

Then we moved to South Florida, built a beautiful house, and, in less than two years, Hurricane Andrew ravaged that home, requiring us to rebuild.

Yes, nature caused those problems, but the house in Connecticut had old wiring, no lightning rod, and no gas generator or solar power collectors. The house in Florida had no hurricane shutters. I did not take steps to prevent those problems.

In my spiritual life, I need preventive measures of prayer and Bible study. I cannot rely on old connections to God or past faithfulness. Staying faithful shields me from storms and keeps the connection to God strong.

LOVIN' FROM THE LORD

Then he said, "This is what I will do: I will tear down my barns and build larger ones, and there I will store all my grain and my goods."
LUKE 12:18

God gave the Israelites all the manna they needed, but told them not hoard it or try to store it up. The Israelites faced moldy manna when they disobeyed and greedily tried to take too much and save it. It became wormy and smelled foul.

In the New Testament, Jesus spoke about another greedy person who planned to build larger barns to store grain (see Luke 12:16–21). This already wealthy man wanted earthly treasure. Jesus used that example to talk about being generous and storing up heavenly treasure of good deeds that cannot be destroyed or stolen.

Thankfully, God wastes nothing. He used moldy bread as a lesson. He uses our sins to teach us and help us become stronger when we turn back to Him.

When mold grows, it appears to be worthless and smelly, ready to be

---

FOOD FOR THOUGHT

When has greed cost you?

When has God used the mold in your life to do something amazing?

---

tossed out. Yet the bacteria in mold are an important source of medicine. Sir Alexander Fleming studied mold for years, eventually developing penicillin, a great healing medicine. He worked diligently, carefully examining the mold under a microscope and recording everything he observed.

God carefully observes us, noting every detail. Nothing escapes God's notice. In our lives, there may be times when things go wrong or when we feel useless. Thankfully, God does not respond, "Too much mold, out you go!"

Instead, God tells us in Romans 8:28 that everything works together for good. God can and will use this mold to bring about healing in our lives, and then He will use us to heal others through our molding experiences.

LOVIN' FROM THE OVEN

My Southern friends helped me find a great Southern biscuit recipe. I tried out a few before settling on what worked best. My mother-in-law grew up in Mississippi and made biscuits with buttermilk. I find that ingredient produces light, fluffy ones that are eaten too fast to ever get moldy.

The Civil War biscuits help prevent mold because you can refrigerate the dough and only bake the number of biscuits needed. To keep bread safe from mold, store it in a dark place at room temperature. You can also double bag or wrap bread tightly in high-quality plastic wrap and freeze it.

BUTTERMILK AND SOUR CREAM BISCUITS

Ingredients

    4 cups unbleached self-rising flour

    1 16-ounce container sour cream

    1/2 cup buttermilk

Directions

Heat oven to 450°F. Place flour in bowl. Blend in enough sour cream with a fork or your hands until the dough leaves sides of bowl. Add buttermilk to form soft dough.

Turn dough onto lightly floured surface. Knead 2 to 3 times. Roll dough to 1/2 or 3/4 inch thickness. Cut round circles with a floured 2- or 3-inch biscuit cutter or open end of a drinking glass. Place on a baking sheet lightly greased with shortening, with biscuit sides touching for soft biscuits; leave them 1 inch apart for crispier sides.

Bake 10–12 minutes.

Optional: Stir in 1/2 cup shredded cheese for cheesy biscuits. Sprinkle with black pepper for additional flavor for cheese biscuits.

MONA'S CIVIL WAR BISCUITS

These biscuits (also called angel biscuits) have been updated to use self-rising flour, but the recipe is based on one from the American Civil War era. The dough can be made ahead and stored in the refrigerator for a few weeks. My friend Mona is from West Virginia and she grew up enjoying this recipe that her mother cooked frequently.

Ingredients

5 cups self-rising flour

1/3 cup sugar

1 teaspoon baking soda

2 packages active dry yeast

1/4 cup warm water

1/2 cup shortening or

   vegetable oil

2 cups buttermilk

Directions

Dissolve yeast in warm water. Sift flour, soda, and sugar together in large bowl. Blend in shortening. Add yeast mixture and buttermilk and mix well. Cover bowl and store in refrigerator to use as needed.

When ready to bake, heat oven to 400°F. Pull off enough dough for the number of biscuits needed. Cut biscuits out on lightly floured surface (don't twist the cutter). Place biscuits on greased pan and bake until lightly browned, about 10 minutes (no need to wait for dough to rise).

JELLY SPOOFS

My children always liked a special treat with leftover biscuits. We cut them open, placed them in a small pan, added a pat of butter and spooned on some jelly. Then we toasted them in the toaster oven.

A MORSEL OF BREAD

Moldy bread led scientists
to the healing power of penicillin.

CHAPTER 45

Burnt Offerings

You shall present these to the LORD at your appointed times,
besides your votive offerings and your freewill offerings,
for your burnt offerings and for your grain offerings
and for your drink offerings and for your peace offerings.

NUMBERS 29:39

I "BURN TOAST" TOO OFTEN, making mistakes because I get distracted and over-committed. I even bought a special toaster oven to stop when the toast is ready, but it still needs my attention or it blackens. One incident taught me to be more intentional about my time commitments, so I won't burn out.

I had casually promised to be in two places, thirty miles apart, simultaneously teaching crafts to girls at camp and directing the children's church Christmas shop. We changed the time for the girls, and I breathed easier. The next day, I glanced at the garbage stacked outside. Later, I panicked at the sound of the garbage truck, as I remembered silver bags next to garbage cans. My son had dutifully taken out every bag—including the ones filled with craft supplies for the weekend activities.

I drove to the dump and pulled in ahead of the truck. While I moved to the indicated spot workers quizzed me about my loss, guessing everything from a diamond ring to a winning lottery ticket. I gingerly stepped into muck, fearing I would land in slime, broken glass, and rotting food. Finally, out tumbled two ripped, silver bags from the truck. I held my thumbs up and grabbed the bags.

The men yelled, "Pine cones?!"

I looked at the surrounding pine trees and replied, "These are special, huge pine cones for children to decorate as Christmas trees." They laughed.

That Christmas, my glowing younger daughter Darlene gave me three large pinecone trees, saying, "Mommy loves pine cones." They still decorate the nativity set and remind me to pray before committing my time.

We should carefully pray before making plans. We should also offer our days and actions to God. Then we'll be energized and not overwhelmed, able to give our best effort to our commitments and focus on what we're doing.

LOVIN' FROM THE LORD

Solomon went up there before the LORD to the bronze altar which was
at the tent of meeting, and offered a thousand burnt offerings on it.
2 CHRONICLES 1:6

Solomon stood over the altar for hours, offering many sacrifices. God surprised him in return by offering to give him anything he desired. Solomon asked for and received great wisdom. God responds to our labors of love for Him. He also knows we get tired.

Jesus understands weariness. He tried to go to a quiet place to rest with His disciples, but crowds followed. He felt compassion for the crowd and stopped to teach them. He felt compassion for their hunger. Jesus responded to the people's offering of their time in listening to Him.

He tested His disciples, who felt stressed and overwhelmed by the thought of feeding so many people. They lacked ability and resources, but Andrew had met a boy willing to share a small lunch. Jesus used the lunch and satisfied everyone as He multiplied bread. He has all the answers we need, even when we are overwhelmed. Without time or money, Jesus reacted FAST.

> **FOOD FOR THOUGHT**
>
> When have you acted FAST on God's call?
>
> What answers has God given you lately?

Felt compassion.

Accepted the available resources

Stepped out in faith

Trusted and **T**hanked His Father.

He knew that a good meal revives us. He gives us fresh bread, not burnt, in exchange for the little we willingly give.

LOVIN' FROM THE OVEN

On busy days, it's easier to pull out refrigerator rolls and biscuits than make my own. They're versatile and easy to cook. I find I'm less likely to burn them because they cook fast and I have less time to get distracted.

FILLED DINNER RING

Ingredients

    1 tube crescent rolls or rectangles of dough

    Your favorite fully cooked fillings: (diced ham and cheese, sloppy Joe, pulled pork, chicken potpie filling)

Instructions

    Heat oven to 400°F. On a greased pan, lay out four rectangles in a cross shape with the center empty. Lay four more rectangles in an X-shape on top of the cross.

Place filling on dough near center hole. Bring ends of rectangles up and over filling. Seal edges to make a closed ring. Bake 10–15 minutes until brown and bubbly.

DESSERT TURNOVER

Ingredients

1 can crescent rolls
Your favorite fillings:
Jelly, Chocolate
chips, Pie filling

Instructions

Heat oven to 400°F. Open crescent rolls and place on greased baking sheet. Spoon filling in center of rolls; overlap ends to cover filling. Bake 10 minutes.

APPLE PIE FILLING

Ingredients

3 apples, peeled and chopped
1/4 cup sugar
1 tablespoon cinnamon

Instructions

Stir all ingredients together in microwave-safe bowl. Microwave on high for 3 minutes. Drain excess juice.

A MORSEL OF BREAD

Be intentional and make choices prayerfully.
You'll have better outcomes.

CHAPTER 46

Rocky Rolls

Or what man is there among you who,
when his son asks for a loaf, will give him a stone?
MATTHEW 7:9

EMOTIONAL PAIN CAN FEEL as if someone has hit us with a large stone. Later, when the tears clear and the pain passes, we often discover an unpolished gemstone or hidden geode, a gift packaged a little differently than the answer we sought.

When a loved one dies, grief can overwhelm us. Thankfully, these days we have changed a funeral to a celebration of life. When my Grandpa Doody died, people set up tables and chairs all over the yard, knowing that hundreds of people would come to the house after the burial to offer sympathy and celebrate his life. People brought casseroles and countless loaves of bread because Grandma had always given bread as gifts. We celebrated Grandpa's life and faith. Over the years, I have shared many stories of my grandparents and great-grandparents. They blessed me with treasured times and gemstones of wisdom.

My friend Betsy died a few years ago. She and her husband Hank had served with Officer's Christian Fellowship at the US Coast Guard Academy. Betsy made bread weekly for many years for the cadets and visitors. For her celebration of life, people baked her recipe of sourdough bread. They filled the room with one hundred loaves and watched a video about her life. She had shared Christ with many people and touched so many lives.

We may place a gravestone on a grave, but it's not just a declaration of death; it's also a marker of a life that left treasured memories. When life seems to give you a stone, ask God to show you the hidden crystals that will add sparkle to your life . . . and be thankful.

LOVIN' FROM THE LORD

The tempter came and said to Him, "If You are the Son of God, command that these stones become bread."

MATTHEW 4:3

Just as it takes time and pressure for coal to be transformed into a diamond, so time and the pressures of pain slowly change us. Somewhere along the way, the diamond emerges, perhaps still uncut and rough edged, but valuable.

Jesus stood in the wilderness surrounded by dirt and stones. It all looked as dry as His mouth. The devil tempted Him to turn the stones to bread. Satan knew God could do anything. But Jesus would not fall prey to such a test. He trusted His Father. He treasured us much more than food. He wanted to obey His Father perfectly to redeem us, and

---

FOOD FOR THOUGHT

What are you thankful for this week?

When have you clung to Scripture while being tempted?

turning stones into bread to satisfy His momentary hunger was not part of the plan.

Responding with Scripture was a great weapon to use against Satan, but it was also a great tool to fill His soul. It's also a great reminder that, when life is hard and the road seems rocky, we can rely on Scripture and cling to God too. After Satan left Jesus, God sent angels to minister to Him. God sends us help, too, so look around and be thankful for the good gifts and people God sends.

LOVIN' FROM THE OVEN

Garlic is a member of the lily family. It has a powerful, pungent flavor when raw that mellows when cooked. It adds zest and a savory taste to food, including bread. It's hard when raw but becomes buttery when roasted. It also provides several health benefits. People in our lives can be powerful, almost pungent, and yet add zest to our lives. Like garlic, they leave an impression long after they pass on to heaven.

PULL-APART GARLIC ROLLS

Use one-quarter of the risen whole wheat dough from this book (page 33) or refrigerated biscuit dough to make these rolls.

Ingredients

    1 tube refrigerated biscuits or one 1/4 of the risen Honey-of-an-Egg
       whole wheat bread dough

    3 tablespoons melted butter

    2 teaspoons grated garlic (or 1 teaspoon garlic powder)

    2 tablespoons fresh minced parsley

    1 cup shredded mozzarella

    Paper muffin liners

Directions

Heat oven to 375°F. Cut or tear biscuits into fourths (or pull chunks of dough) and place in mixing bowl. Add remaining ingredients. Mix by hand, coating all the pieces of dough. Place paper muffin liners in the tins. Place pieces in muffin tin, about 3 chunks per tin (3/4 full).

Bake for 15 minutes (5 minutes longer with whole wheat dough). Makes 12 biscuits.

Options:

Glaze hot rolls with warm pizza sauce.
Mix in chopped bacon or pepperoni for pizza rolls.

A MORSEL OF BREAD

When you face hard times, be ready
for God to send ministering angels.

CHAPTER 47

Bread Scraps

So they gathered them up, and filled twelve baskets
with fragments from the five barley loaves
which were left over by those who had eaten.

JOHN 6:13

MY HUSBAND, JIM, had spent much of the morning helping to cook eggs Benedict for Mother's Day for all the moms and their families at church. Our family had eaten and returned home a few hours earlier. Jim didn't have a job, so the men decided he should take the bulk of the leftovers. Jim arrived home with boxes of goodies: two cases of English muffins, one case of eggs, bags of Canadian bacon, and other supplies for me to store and use. I gave some to a writer friend. Our children all enjoyed a week of English muffin and egg dishes. I froze some of the English muffins so they wouldn't get stale.

Bread goes stale because the starch in the bread changes to a crystalline form, reacting to the water in the bread. That process speeds up at cooler temperatures, but freezing bread traps the moisture as ice and preserves bread.

Leftovers challenge the cook to be creative while providing an opportunity for sharing and saving money. The men at church understood our needs and blessed us. Those days of tight finances increased our own compassion for people in need. I've developed a habit of looking around to find items I'm not using to give to shelters and food pantries. My leftovers become useful resources for others.

LOVIN' FROM THE LORD

Do you not yet understand or remember the five loaves of the five thousand, and how many baskets full you picked up? Or the seven loaves of the four thousand, and how many large baskets full you picked up?
MATTHEW 16:9–10

Jesus could have multiplied just the right amount of bread for the crowd, but He supplied more. The disciples filled baskets with leftover fragments. People tore apart the bread, so that left ragged-edged pieces.

We don't know how the disciples used the leftovers. We do know that a remark Jesus made about leaven in bread made them wonder if He knew they had forgotten to bring bread. Jesus turned and asked them how much bread they'd collected each time He'd multiplied a few loaves. Then He said He was not speaking about bread, but about the sin of the Pharisees.

His words reminded them that the Son of God did not have to worry about bread. His focus is not on food and filling stomachs, but on changing hearts. Jesus used miracles to illustrate deeper truths. Bread in the Bible is more than food. It illustrates God's provision, covenant, and relationship

---

FOOD FOR THOUGHT

What is your favorite Scripture passage on bread?

When have you been challenged to be creative?

---

with people. The leaven He mentioned in that case represented the fermenting of hearts with sin, the staleness of minds in not taking a fresh look at Scripture.

Passages on bread should challenge us to take a new look and share our insights.

LOVIN' FROM THE OVEN

In Serbia, it is unthinkable to toss out old bread. Customs to use the bread include hanging it in bags on the side of dumpsters for homeless people. And it is acceptable for the poor to ask for leftover bread in bakeries. There are many great uses for day-old bread.

CROUTONS

Heat oven to 400°F. Cube the bread and toast it to make crunchy croutons. If the bread is too hard, moisten it with water. Dump cubes in a bowl and drizzle with Italian dressing or olive oil and your choice of seasonings. Bake until crispy.

ITALIAN BREAD SALAD OR PANZANELLA

Ingredients

2 large, ripe tomatoes, cut into bite-size pieces

1 cucumber, diced

1 bell pepper, seeded and chopped

2 scallions, chopped

1 clove garlic, very finely minced

1/2 cup fresh basil leaves, chopped

1/2 cup extra virgin olive oil, plus more as needed

3 tablespoons balsamic vinegar

Salt and pepper

8 slices thick, stale, country-style Italian bread, torn into bite-size pieces

Directions

If bread is quite stale and dry, sprinkle water over the bread and let it soak, then hand-press excess water out and let sit on a paper towel.

In a bowl, combine the tomatoes, cucumber, pepper, scallions, garlic, and basil for the filling. Drizzle with olive oil and vinegar. Season with salt and pepper and toss well. Place half of the bread in a wide, shallow bowl. Spoon half of the filling over the bread. Layer the remaining bread on top and then the remaining filling mixture.

Cover and refrigerate for at least one hour. Just before serving, toss the salad. If bread is too dry, add more olive oil.

LAYERED BEEF AND STALE BREAD CASSEROLE

Ingredients

8 slices stale bread	1/2 teaspoon oregano
1/2 cup butter	1 cup shredded cheddar cheese
1/2 pound ground beef	1 egg, slightly beaten
1/2 cup chopped scallions	3/4 cup milk
2 tablespoons celery, diced	Paprika
1/2 teaspoon salt	

Directions

Heat oven to 350°F. Toast bread, then butter on both sides. Brown meat, scallions, and celery. Add salt and oregano. Grease a 9x9-inch baking pan. In pan, alternate layers of bread, meat, and cheese. Mix egg, milk, and salt; pour over layers. Sprinkle with paprika. Bake 30–35 minutes.

A MORSEL OF BREAD

You may only have a scrap to share,
but when it's added to what others offer,
it's more than enough.

CHAPTER 48

Worse Than Stale Bread

The bowl of flour was not exhausted nor did the jar of oil
become empty, according to the word of the LORD
which He spoke through Elijah.

1 KINGS 17:16

"MOM, THIS CEREAL TASTES STALE."

"I don't like this cereal anymore. Can you buy a different kind?"

My little cherubs often left portions of cereal in the box. Thankfully, my friend Anne gave me her recipe for cereal muffins. It called for a full package of bran cereal, but I changed the recipe to use combinations of leftover cereal. We called it garbage bread. I'd also add in chopped dried fruit or nuts. I used to store leftover cereal in a container in the freezer until I'd collected enough to make the batter. The recipe seemed to make an unlimited supply. I would scoop out what I needed for the number of muffins requested and bake them on chilly mornings.

Girlfriends and sharing recipes go together. Anne and I chatted online recently about how neither of us had used the recipe in years. My children are grown, and we both live in warmer climates now and she and her husband retired. She's used my Honey-of-an-Egg Whole Wheat Bread recipe for decades. We share lots of memories. I stitched hems of of her bridesmaid's gowns. When my sister-in-law decided to have her wedding in Anne's hometown, Anne connected us with her florist friend. Memories and friendships last much longer than the foods we prepare. Pulling out a recipe often brings up images of a friend's smile or other treasured memories. God's bounty is limitless.

God provided a widow with a jar that never emptied. He also provides us with recipes to help our budgets and more importantly, provides us with lasting friendships.

LOVIN' FROM THE LORD

But [the widow of Zarephath] said, "As the LORD your God lives,
I have no bread, only a handful of flour in the bowl and a little oil
in the jar; and behold, I am gathering a few sticks that I may go in
and prepare for me and my son, that we may eat it and die."

1 KINGS 17:12

What's worse than stale bread? What more could go wrong when we come to a time of drought than stale bread or stale cereal? One widow in the Old Testament discovered the answer. A severe drought had led to such a shortage that no wheat grew for flour to make the bread. Totally depleted and drained, this widow was preparing to die when she met God's man, the prophet Elijah.

The widow remains nameless. Her story could happen to anyone. We all can get to such drained,

FOOD FOR THOUGHT

How has God provided
for you this week?

How has God used you
to provide for the needs
of others?

strained times of drought that we feel we have reached the end of our resources. This is when we are ready to let go of ourselves and let God provide. This poor woman had prepared to cook one last meal. As she gathered sticks, Elijah showed up and asked for water.

She brought the water, and he confidently asked for bread. She explained her circumstance to him. He told her God would provide if she made the first bread cake for him. The widow obeyed Elijah, and her oil and flour never ran out during the remainder of the three-year drought!

She is known as the widow of Zarephath, a word that means refinement. Her story continued as God refined her heart. When her son died, she complained to Elijah, who restored the boy's life. She realized that God had sent Elijah, who spoke truth. God provided life when there appeared to be nothing but dryness and death.

LOVIN' FROM THE OVEN

Anne and I have been friends for many years, since before our weddings. We both chat about how we have used recipes the other shared for decades now.

ANNE STOPPE'S SIX-WEEK CEREAL MUFFINS (GARBAGE BREAD)

Ingredients

15-ounce box bran cereal with
  raisins (7 1/2 cups)
5 cups flour
5 teaspoons baking soda
2 teaspoons salt
4 eggs, beaten

1 cup melted shortening
3 cups sugar
1 quart buttermilk
  (find buttermilk with a long
  expiration date)

Directions

Mix cereal with dry ingredients in large mixing bowl. Add eggs, short-ening, and buttermilk and mix well. Store in covered container in refrigerator and use as desired for muffins.

When ready to bake

Heat oven to 400°F. Fill greased muffin cups 2/3 full.
Bake 15–20 minutes.

Tips

- This batter stores in the refrigerator for up to 6 weeks, tightly sealed.
- The recipe makes a lot. To make a smaller batch, divide by four, using just under 2 cups of cereal.
- It works well with crisp rice cereal, oat cereal, granola, cornflakes, or a mix of them.
- If using a chunkier cereal, crush or grind it loosely.

A MORSEL OF BREAD

Make plans for using leftovers.
Make plans, too, to spend
extra time with loved ones.

CHAPTER 49

Up with Crumbs!

*[The Canaanite woman] said, "Yes, Lord; but even the dogs feed on
the crumbs which fall from their masters' table." Then Jesus said to her,
"O woman, your faith is great; it shall be done for you as you wish."
And her daughter was healed at once.*

MATTHEW 15:27–28

INSTEAD OF NICE, FRESH BREAD, daily life often falls apart into a pile of breadcrumbs. This leaves lots of tiny pieces, but little peace!

Before leaving town, Jim asked me to take our van to the auto shop. Rebecca followed behind in our little Subaru. Alas, the van broke down on the way, with a split radiator hose. Rebecca drove on to the auto shop for help and returned to wait with me in the hot August sun for the tow. Then, the Subaru's battery died! After a charge from a helpful motorist, we returned home, wilted and thirsty.

I filled the battery with water. Despite the puddle of water left behind, I managed to get the car to a shop, buy a battery, and return home! My sons quickly learned how to install a car battery.

I looked for a crumb from God's Word and read about a woman

happy to receive crumbs in the midst of a serious family health need. I thanked God for my healthy family.

The mechanic called. The van had a clogged radiator and needed additional repairs. The vacuum cleaner and video camera both broke, and a toilet overflowed. We prayed over each problem, read how to fix things, and the children helped with repairs.

Before the account of the woman and crumbs, Jesus said that what comes out of our mouths comes from the heart. The Canaanite woman kept speaking on faith. Instead of complaining, I thanked God for bright, faithful children and all the repairs we had accomplished.

LOVIN' FROM THE LORD

[The Canaanite woman] answered and said to Him, "Yes, Lord, but even the dogs under the table feed on the children's crumbs."

MARK 7:28

Again, God reminded me of a woman thankful for crumbs. This event is recorded in both Matthew 15:21–28 and Mark 7:24–30. Any event recorded twice needs to be looked at carefully!

Jesus conversed with a Canaanite woman who asked for His help. Jesus told her that the children's bread is not to be thrown to the dogs. The Canaanites, who refused passage to the Israelites after they left Egypt, had remained longtime enemies of the Jews. The woman boldly replied that dogs feed on the crumbs that fall from the table. Her daughter suffered terribly, and she believed His "crumbs" would be enough for her. Jesus marveled at her great faith.

FOOD FOR THOUGHT

Do you praise God daily, especially when problems crumble your plans?

What little blessings are you thankful for today?

Crumbs are useful in cooking for a crunchy topping for casseroles, binding ground beef or seafood for patties and meatballs, creating sweet bread puddings, and thickening stew. For life, I need only to remember that one little crumb from the Bread of Life can meet my needs!

Throughout that crazy time of car problems and household repairs, God kept us safe and provided needed help. He even provided funds to cover the problems. It is in discovering the power of a crumb from God that I am humbly reminded of His greatness.

LOVIN' FROM THE OVEN

As I became an empty nester and widow, I experimented on baking for one person. This comes from some experiments I tried after checking out other bread pudding recipes.

CHOCOLATE
BREAD PUDDING IN A MUG

Ingredients

1 teaspoon butter

1/4 cup bread crumbs

1 egg

2 tablespoons sugar

1/3 cup milk

1 tablespoon chocolate chips, chopped apple, or berries

1/4 teaspoon cinnamon (optional)

Directions

Melt butter in a microwave-safe mug and stir in breadcrumbs.

Crack egg in a small bowl; add sugar and beat well. Add milk and stir. Mix in chocolate chips, chopped apple, or berries. Add cinnamon if desired. Pour mixture over mug of breadcrumbs. Microwave on high for 2 minutes.

Let sit 30 seconds. If too runny, microwave another 30 seconds; repeat this step as needed until set. Cool about 5 minutes.

Tips for Using Bread Crumbs

- DIY breadcrumbs: process stale or toasted bread in a food processer until it forms fine crumbs. Add flavors as desired (dried oregano, basil, parsley, thyme). Store in re-sealable bag up to six months in freezer.
- For a crunchy topping, mix 1 cup breadcrumbs with 1–2 tablespoons olive oil. Sprinkle over casserole.
- Mix breadcrumbs with one small package seasoned dry salad dressing mix (ranch, Italian). Use for coating chicken or fish for frying.
- For baked cheeseballs, mix 1 cup breadcrumbs, 2 cups grated cheddar cheese, and 1 cup butter in a food processor. Roll into one-inch balls. Bake at 350°F until lightly browned.

A MORSEL OF BREAD

When life gives you bread crumbs,
learn to bake casseroles.

Bread from Heaven

God sent dreams of bread to a few individuals. These dreams served as calls to action and change for those people. God reminds us that He provides much more than mere edible bread. He provides plans and dreams for us to follow. That's part of our manna from heaven.

CHAPTER 50

Dreams of Wheat and Bread

[Joseph] said to [his brothers], "Listen to this dream I had:
We were binding sheaves of grain out in the field when suddenly
my sheaf rose and stood upright, while your sheaves
gathered around mine and bowed down to it."
GENESIS 37:6–7 NIV

I DREAMED OF A HUGE, WONDERFUL LOAF of golden bread. Suddenly, it crumbled, and God said, "I called My people to be one bread, and they have made it into bread crumbs." That image has stayed with me; I can still close my eyes and picture it. Another time, God gave me a dream of bread that kept growing larger and multiplied. I prayed the next morning and realized that it reflected Jesus, the Bread of Life.

When I realized God wanted me to become a writer, I went to a retreat and prayed. God gave me a vision. It looked as though His hand was cupped with a river of water flowing over it. It held what looked like a golden ball. I said, "So, You want me to write a book?"

God replied, "No."

"So, I'm off the hook, and You don't want me to write?"

God replied, "No."

"Then what do You want?"

"This is a seed. Plant it, and it will produce much."

God wanted me to be a writer, but not of just one book.

The next morning, I took time choosing where to sit for breakfast at the retreat. After we ate, the leader told us to turn over the placemats. We each found a unique painting. Mine depicted my dream, with Proverbs 3:4–5 on it. I started writing, and the picture hangs in my office. I think of the seed as a golden seed of wheat.

LOVIN' FROM THE LORD

Now do not be grieved or angry with yourselves,
because you sold me [Joseph] here,
for God sent me before you [his brothers] to preserve life.
GENESIS 45:5

I loved driving through miles of golden wheat when I lived in the Midwest. Watching it sway in the breeze always reminded me of Joseph's vision and story in the Old Testament. God used grain, brothers, dreams, famine, and an abundance of wheat to remind His people that His purpose would triumph and that He has the power to deliver His people.

Jacob's favoritism of one son, Joseph, caused hurt feelings and long-term problems with his other children. To add to the brothers' pain, God appeared to favor

---

FOOD FOR THOUGHT

What have others done to hurt you that God turned around for your good?

How do you keep from playing favorites?

Joseph, too, when He gave him a dream that indicated Joseph would rule over his brothers. The hurt took root in the men and grew into resentment and anger that led to sin.

God gave Joseph a dream, a vision of the future, in symbolic images. Joseph saw twelve sheaves of wheat, representing himself and his eleven brothers. A sheaf is an omer, or about two quarts, of wheat stalks bound together. A sheaf represented a generous quantity. Thus, God had blessed all twelve with abundance. However, eleven sheaves bowed to Joseph's sheaf, symbolizing honor to Joseph and a position of authority over his brothers. Perhaps he told his dream at the wrong time or to the wrong people, but it angered his brothers, and they sold Joseph into slavery.

Too often, we are not content with what we have and resent God for blessing other people. Joseph's family reunited over famine and the wheat Joseph had wisely stored. Joseph forgave his brothers and told them that, although they had meant it for evil, God had meant it for good to save His people.

LOVIN' FROM THE OVEN

God uses dreams because they provide powerful images. Art recreates images seen. Enjoy creating some art with dough. The first time I did this, I made bread dough into Christmas wreaths and used them as centerpieces.

BREAD DOUGH ART

Ingredients
> 2 cups flour
> 1/2 cup salt
> 3/4 cup water

Directions

Mix all ingredients together by hand until it develops a good plastic consistency. Knead for 5–10 minutes. If dough is sticky, knead in more flour.

Pinch, roll, and shape dough into desired shapes or roll it and use cookie cutters to shape it. Add decorative touches such as pressing with tines of a fork (Note: too detailed of a pattern will not hold).

Add hanger if desired: press a paper clip into back.

Bake at 300°F for about 2 hours or leave in sunny windowsill about 3 days to dry.

Paint with acrylic polymer paint. Allow paint to completely dry, then coat with Shellac.

A MORSEL OF BREAD

Dough can be molded into art
that can be preserved,
just as we can be molded into
the people God wants us to be,
preserved by His grace.

CHAPTER 51

Storing Grain

So [Joseph] gathered all the food of these seven years which occurred
in the land of Egypt and placed the food in the cities;
he placed in every city the food from its own surrounding fields.

GENESIS 41:48

A FRIEND WITH A GREAT HEART for helping hungry families directs a food pantry. She carefully stores foods and watches expiration dates. When she heard about a child who had not eaten for a day, she filled a bag and drove to the family's home. She delivered to the mother bread, rice, cereal, milk, and other staples. The woman cried when she received the food. Her husband had recently lost his job, and they had nothing to eat. My friend explained how the food pantry worked and gave the woman the address and a phone number. She finds new families in need almost every week. The pantry is located at the back of a church that provided storage room.

Recently, another church that has a food pantry in the back started an after-school program for needy families. The after-care director works with the food pantry coordinator to provide a snack for the children when they arrive.

Programs to help the needy are replicated across the country and demonstrate how the body of Christ works together. Volunteers often have connections with area bakeries and grocers to pick up day-old bread and other supplies before dates expire. Healthy communities and churches work together to help a community thrive when they include people who create programs for people in need.

LOVIN' FROM THE LORD

Joseph stored grain in great abundance like the sand of the sea;
until he stopped measuring it, for it was beyond measure.
GENESIS 41:49

After slavery and prison, Joseph rose to a position of power in Egypt. He supervised and planned the grain storage for Pharaoh to prepare for the coming famine that God had revealed in a dream to Pharaoh (Genesis 41:15–36). Joseph's wise handling of grain saved many people, including his own family. It also provided the opportunity for reconciliation with his brothers.

Isolating grain within each city that grew wheat probably helped preserve it and spare it from pestilence. If one area had an infestation, keeping it isolated also contained the insects. They probably used clay jars sealed with mud, called *pithos*. Grain silos were plaster-coated enclosures. They poured the grain in the top and a little door at the bottom opened to disperse the grain.

> ### FOOD FOR THOUGHT
>
> What dreams do you think God has given you?
>
> How does God help you discern truth?

Pharaoh called Joseph the wisest and most discerning man he knew because God made known to Joseph what Pharaoh's dreams meant. Pharaoh recognized the power of God to give people wisdom, even in plans about food.

LOVIN' FROM THE OVEN

A gift of ingredients in jars with a recipe has become a special way to pass on a treat. The person just adds a few things and makes it, without the chemicals in prepared mixes.

BREAD GIFTS AND RECIPE JARS

To assemble
1. Measure the basic dry ingredients of a recipe.
2. Layer ingredients in a Mason jar or other container that is airtight.
3. Write out what to add and steps to prepare the bread.
4. Decorate the container with ribbon.

CINNAMON NUT MUFFIN MIX IN A JAR

Layer the following ingredients in a jar in order:
1. 2 cups flour
2. 2 teaspoons baking powder
3. 1/2 teaspoon baking soda
4. 3/4 cup sugar
5. 1/2 tablespoon ground cinnamon
6. 1/4 teaspoon ground nutmeg
7. 1/4 teaspoon ground ginger
8. 1/4 teaspoon ground cloves
9. 1/2 teaspoon salt
10. 1/4 cup chopped roasted nuts (chocolate chips, dried cherries, blueberries, other fruit)
11. Combine 1/2 cup brown sugar and 1/2 cup flour and put in a small, resealable bag. Place it on top of the other ingredients in the jar.

Then, add a package of paper muffin liners on top of jar and decorate jar as desired. Print or write directions that follow and attach that to the jar.

Directions for baking

Heat oven to 400°F. Set aside sealed bag. Empty jar into bowl.

Mix in 1/4 cup oil, 1 cup milk, 1 teaspoon vanilla, and 1 egg. Place muffin liners in tin. Fill muffin cups 2/3 full.

For crumble topping, shake baggie and pour in small bowl; mix in 1/4 cup softened butter; sprinkle mixture on top of batter.

Bake for 15 minutes or until toothpick inserted in center comes out clean.

Tips for Adapting Recipes to a Jar Gift

- Try adapting a recipe for this use. You can adapt the pumpkin bread recipe from chapter 24 for use in a jar gift. See page 107 for a complete ingredient list and instructions. Layer all the dry ingredients in the jar. Cover a can of pumpkin pie filling with colored paper. Add directions. The individual will need to add eggs and oil.
- Jar gifts work well for recipes that don't use too many liquid ingredients.

A MORSEL OF BREAD

A gift of bread
is a gift from the heart.

CHAPTER 52

Gideon's Bread Dream and Victory

When Gideon came, behold, a man was relating
a dream to his friend. And he said, "Behold, I had a dream;
a loaf of barley bread was tumbling into the camp of Midian,
and it came to the tent and struck it so that it fell,
and turned it upside down so that the tent lay flat."

JUDGES 7:13

DREAMS CAN MOTIVATE US. The call to writing stayed in my heart, and I wrote in a journal that I would study and give God all my effort for five years. If I didn't get anything published, I would know I had misunderstood.

One of the first rejections I received included a form that listed reasons for rejections. My form was filled with check marks. This gave me hope. I had a checklist to follow! My husband rolled his eyes when I told him I would write something they could not check off. I worked for a few months and submitted my new piece. I received an acceptance.

In time, I had more pieces accepted than rejected. Then the editor of a magazine I wrote for on a regular basis called and asked me to write a book.

God's call and the dreams He puts in our hearts and minds inspire us to reach beyond ourselves. I studied math, not English, in college. I felt like Gideon, the least likely person to be published. I had barley flour as my ingredient for books instead of the refined flour of those who'd studied journalism or creative writing. I prayed Hebrews 13:20–21, that God would equip me for doing His will. He equipped me through conferences and books on writing. He sent a walking partner, a published author, to mentor me.

> **FOOD FOR THOUGHT**
>
> When have you asked God to confirm something?
>
> When has God handled your battles?

When God calls us to do something, the desire remains with us, and He often confirms it with opened doors of opportunity. The calling will align with Scripture and be beneficial to others. Dare to ask God to give you dreams and pray that He will equip you and give you opportunities.

LOVIN' FROM THE LORD

His friend replied, "This [dream of bread] is nothing less than the sword of Gideon the son of Joash, a man of Israel; God has given Midian and all the camp into his hand."

JUDGES 7:14

During the night, God told Gideon to go to the enemy's camp. Gideon took his servant Purah, and they snuck into the camp in the darkness. In our darkest moments, against all odds, God sends us encouragement. Gideon overheard a dream being discussed that gave him courage. In the dream, barley, a grain inferior to wheat, represented Gideon and his inferior little band, not worth much notice in the eyes of military leaders. But with God's power, these commandos outmaneuvered and overpowered the vast army of Midianites.

When Purah overheard about the dream, he said it was "the sword of Gideon" and thus depicted the bread that flattened a tent into a symbol for victory. Gideon then bowed and worshiped God.

Gideon took action fast. He returned to his camp and called out for the men to get up. After all the threshing and sifting of Gideon and his men, the little band had transformed into a unified team that sustained life, a wholesome loaf that smashed the enemy. The battle is described in Judges 7:16–25. Gideon used the noise of trumpets and shouts to confuse the enemy.

The Lord set the enemy soldiers against one another—the Israelites had to do little fighting to win. Gideon's warriors called out, "A sword for the LORD and for Gideon!" and triumphed against all odds.

LOVIN' FROM THE OVEN

While studying Old Testament stories and seeing many references to barley bread, I decided to try making some. I prefer the ones cooked in oil, as that adds more flavor and can change depending on the type of oil used.

BARLEY FLATBREAD

Ingredients
 1 cup barley flour
 1/2 cup water
 1 tablespoon honey
 1/4 teaspoon salt

Directions

Mix flour and salt in a large bowl. Stir in the water and honey to form a fairly stiff dough (it will not be smooth).

Turn dough out onto a countertop and knead for a few minutes until it becomes smooth. Set a griddle or large frying pan on the stove over medium-high heat. Pull out 2-inch balls of dough and roll into flat circles.

Gently place each circle of dough on hot griddle and cook for about 2 minutes.

Flip bread over and cook for another minute or two on the second side until you see golden brown patches (the flatbread edges may curl a bit).

Note: If dough tends to stick to pan, use a little oil in the pan.

Serve hot with honey, butter, or yogurt. They are also good with meats and sandwich fillings. Or serve them like a pancake with syrup.

A MORSEL OF BREAD

Even the cheapest flour
can be transformed into tasty bread.

CHAPTER 53

Manna from Heaven

Now the manna was like coriander seed,
and its appearance like that of bdellium.
The people would go about and gather it and grind it
between two millstones or beat it in the mortar,
and boil it in the pot and make cakes with it;
and its taste was as the taste of cakes baked with oil.

NUMBERS 11:7–8

MY CHILDREN HUNTED FOR PENNIES and gathered them up. We sat and talked about how the coins had covered the ground and then read about manna in the Bible. We showed them coriander seeds, and they wondered how much would need to be gathered to make a bread cake or slice of bread.

We looked at grains of wheat and how many fit in a cup. They decided there were too many to count. We looked at oatmeal, which seems like little flakes but is actually hulled oat grains. Then we tried cooking with the oatmeal, making hot cereal, baking oatmeal bars, oatmeal banana bread, and oatmeal cookies.

Various grains are versatile and can be used in many recipes. The Israelites cooked the manna God sent in many ways too. They boiled it like oatmeal and shaped and cooked loaves. Scripture described manna as tasting like honey when fresh or olive oil when cooked. Oatmeal cooked in different ways creates new textures and tastes. That's part of the joy of cooking and modifying recipes.

We connect our children to Scripture when we help them investigate and understand what they read, including the sights, sounds, tastes, and other sensory images described.

LOVIN' FROM THE LORD

Jesus said to them, "Truly, truly I say to you, it is not Moses who has given you the bread out of heaven, but it is my Father who gives you the true bread out of heaven."
JOHN 6:32

After the Israelites left Egypt, they wandered in a desert for forty years. They journeyed with no time or place to grow food. That vast number of people needed nourishment, and God sent it directly from heaven. The people called it manna, which means "what is it?" because it was unknown on earth at that time.

> **FOOD FOR THOUGHT**
>
> When has God poured out a blessing in your life?
>
> What miracles has God done in your life?

Manna became more than bread for stomachs. It became a symbol of God's desire to feed people's souls with His Word. Man is to live a fuller life on the Word of God.

With the death of the generation that left Israel and refused to trust God, the people finally entered the Promised Land. God stopped the manna the day after the people celebrated the first Passover in the Promised Land. While in the wilderness, God had made a covenant with them and had established feasts and offerings. These included manna as a sign of the covenant and grain and bread as offerings. He had laid a foundation to continue His relationship with the people, and it incorporated bread.

When Jesus performed a miracle by multiplying bread, He referred to the manna God the Father had sent. He revealed that manna had fore-shadowed His coming as the Bread of Life. Jesus is the true bread we all need.

LOVIN' FROM THE OVEN

God the Father gave the Israelites a gift of manna. It became a treasured memory with some kept in a jar in the Ark of the Covenant after the manna stopped.

God gave us a greater treasure in giving us Jesus, the Bread of Life. Mary wrapped Jesus in swaddling clothes and let the shepherds see Him. Make little bundles of joy with crescent rolls filled with something tasty as reminders of the swaddling clothes and treasure of Jesus inside.

TREASURES IN A BLANKET

Ingredients

Refrigerated crescent rolls

Mini sausages, olives, or chopped nuts

Directions

Heat oven to 400°F. Open can and roll out dough. Cut into long tri-angle strips; each roll can then be cut into four.

Place filling at long end. Roll dough around filling. Place on baking sheet that is lightly greased with shortening.

Bake for 8–10 minutes until dough is risen and golden.

A MORSEL OF BREAD

A meal becomes a feast when
homemade bread and butter are added.

Feasts of Bread

God's festivals and feasts for Israel included bread and grain and often revolved around the harvesting of grain. God wants us to celebrate and rejoice in His provision. The bounty He provides reminds us to be grateful and to look forward to an eternal celebration in heaven.

CHAPTER 54

Celebration with Bread

Then [Nehemiah] said to [the people in Jerusalem],
"Go, eat of the fat, drink of the sweet, and send portions to him
who has nothing prepared; for this day is holy to our Lord.
Do not be grieved, for the joy of the LORD is your strength."
NEHEMIAH 8:10

I STARTED MAKING CHRISTMAS BREAD years ago, to pass out to neighbors. After he got old enough, my grandson, Joseph, enjoyed helping me. We mixed the fine flour and other ingredients, then let it rise. He punched the dough down, and we rolled it out on the counter. We cut the dough into strips and shaped the bread. For trees, we rounded each strip into a rope and placed a fat one as a trunk on our greased cookie sheet. Then we placed different-sized lengths of dough-rope crosswise over the trunk and curled the ends.

Sometimes, we twisted two ropes together and shaped them like a candy cane. We made a second candy cane and placed the two canes together to form a heart. Other times, we braided three long ropes, formed a circle, and pinched the ends together to form a wreath. We made a thin short rope, shaped it like a bow, and added it to the wreath.

We let the shaped bread rise again and then baked it. When the bread cooled, we drizzled icing on it and decorated it with candied cherries. After all his hard work, Joseph enjoyed giving breads to friends as much as I did.

The Israelites celebrated holy days with feasting. We, too, have special foods and feasting as part of celebrating holy days that help us rejoice and remember the Lord.

LOVIN' FROM THE LORD

All the people went away to eat, to drink, to send portions,
and to celebrate a great festival, because they understood
the words which had been made known to them.

NEHEMIAH 8:12

I usually add a Christmas card with the breads I give. Even two months after my husband died, I made Christmas bread. No matter what else is happening in your life, Christmas is a time to celebrate and rejoice that Jesus came to give us eternal life. It's a time to share God's love.

Ezra had read from the Law. Nehemiah looked at the weeping Israelites and spoke. They cried because they had listened to God's Word and understood it. They realized they had not been following God the way they should. Nehemiah explained that, as they understood and their hearts again turned to God, it was a time to rejoice and find strength in God's

---

FOOD FOR THOUGHT

When has God's Word strengthened and encouraged you?

When have you given food to the poor? Have you ever served in a food kitchen?

Word. He reminded them it was time to restore the Festival of Booths. The feast is described in Leviticus 23, where the people lived in booths made of branches to remember that the Israelites had lived in booths when God freed them from slavery in Egypt.

Part of the celebration included sending portions of food to the poor and celebrating a feast. Nehemiah encouraged them to enjoy fatty and sweet treats. Celebrating should remind us of our many blessings and thus encourage us to give to others.

LOVIN' FROM THE OVEN

I make this large batch of dough so I can make several small Christmas breads to give away. They look festive decorated with green and red cherries. This is a much lighter bread than the Three Kings Bread found in chapter five. It is not filled but simply decorated after baking. In our home, we eat this bread on Christmas morning. The Three Kings Bread is generally eaten on January 6th, for celebrating the Three Kings Day.

CHRISTMAS BREAD

Ingredients

8 cups all-purpose flour, unbleached

2 packages active dry yeast

2 cups milk, warmed

1 cup shortening

1/2 cup sugar

1 teaspoon salt

4 eggs

Directions

Combine 3 cups of the flour with yeast in large bowl and set aside.

In saucepan, heat milk, shortening, sugar, and salt until warm (115–120°F). Add to dry mix. Add eggs. Beat at low speed of electric mixer for 30 seconds to mix.

Beat on high speed for 3 minutes.

By hand, add in as much of the remaining flour as needed to make moderately stiff dough. Place in greased bowl, turn dough to grease all surfaces, then cover it. Let rise till doubled, about 1 hour.

Punch down, cover, let rest ten minutes.

Divide dough in half. Roll each half into a 15x10-inch rectangle.

Cut each rectangle of dough into 15 1-inch strips. Braid and shape dough as desired and place on greased baking pans. Cover and let rise until doubled (about 1 1/2 hours).

Bake at 400°F for 12–15 minutes, until golden.

Cool and drizzle on icing.

Decorate with candied cherries: cut red cherries in half for berries; cut green cherries in fourths for leaves; place two leaves on either side of a cherry to form a holly design.

Shaping bread

- Wreaths: take three strips, braid them and form into a circle for a wreath. Pinch ends together.
- Candy cane hearts: take two strips. Roll each strip to form a rope. Twist them and shape twisted rope into a candy cane shape. Place two candy canes with opposite hooks together to form a heart.
- Trees: lay 1 long 8-inch strip for tree trunk. Cut strips 8, 7, 6, 5, 4, 3, and 2 inches long and place across trunk to form tree.

A MORSEL OF BREAD

Holiday traditions usually
include special breads
that evoke special memories.

CHAPTER 55

Picnic with Jesus

Jesus came and took the bread and gave it to them,
and the fish likewise.

JOHN 21:13

I HELPED TEACH CANOEING at camp. We would paddle out a ways and then glide our canoes close together in a line, sort of rafting up. We'd float together for a while and sometimes enjoy a picnic at sea, eating sandwiches and drinking water. The girls enjoyed the fast pace of paddling on the water, but they also liked the quiet times when we relaxed and enjoyed the scenery and camaraderie of being together.

Picnics are fun, whether with a crowd, family, or just a few friends. My daughter, Darlene, loved holding picnics with friends. She had a special wicker picnic basket she'd fill with crackers and boxed juice or sometimes she'd make sandwiches or take sliced bread and jam. She'd walk behind our home to a little beach that had a picnic table and enjoy private time with a girlfriend.

One year for Mother's Day, she planned a special picnic with one of her friends and invited her friend's mother and me. We enjoyed the treats they had packed. They entertained us with singing and poetry. A gentle breeze kept us cool, and the sounds of nature mixed with our laughter and chatter. That special day of fellowship remains a cherished memory.

Jesus took time for a picnic with His friends. The ordinary day became special with the catch of fish, food cooked over a fire, and the conversation between Jesus and Peter. We can transform an ordinary day into a special event when we invest time in people.

LOVIN' FROM THE LORD

He saith to him again the second time, Simon, son of Jonas,
lovest thou me? He saith unto him, Yea, Lord;
thou knowest that I love thee. He saith unto him, Feed my sheep.
JOHN 21:16 KJV

Peter and some of the disciples went fishing not long after the resurrection. A man called out from shore and asked if they had caught any fish. They answered no. The man told them to cast the net on the other side, and fish immediately filled the net.

John realized the stranger's identity and said, "It is the Lord." Peter then dove into the water and swam to the beach.

Imagine the surprise of the disciples when they arrived ashore and found Jesus had made a charcoal fire and had fish cooking, with bread to complete the meal. Jesus gave them bread, and they shared a breakfast picnic.

FOOD FOR THOUGHT

How can you tend to God's people?

Have you ever needed God's forgiveness but found it hard to accept?

After breakfast, Jesus spoke to Peter and asked him to feed His sheep. He wanted Peter to become a shepherd of people. He had called him to be a fisher of men, someone who would witness and share the gospel message. But now He asked more of Peter. He wanted Peter to become a leader and disciple people.

He also asked Peter three times, "Do you love me?" This illustrated a restoration for the three times Peter had denied Jesus. Jesus is always ready to forgive us and always ready to ask us to do more than follow Him and share the good news. He asked Peter to feed His sheep, to tend His flock, His people. He wants us to lead and disciple others. Breaking bread with Jesus is a time to let Jesus into our hearts and listen to His call.

LOVIN' FROM THE OVEN

Our family enjoyed camping and liked making our tasty bread over hot coals. Spread coals evenly and avoid flames that burn the dough.

PICNIC STICK BREAD

Ingredients
Refrigerated breadstick or biscuit dough
Butter
Toppings: Garlic powder, cinnamon sugar, or parmesan cheese
Long sticks or dowels

Directions
Peel bark off sticks or cover with foil.

Take a breadstick strip (or roll biscuit into long rope) and flatten to make thin strips. Twirl dough around stick, starting at one end; leave other end of stick empty for handle.

Hold over hot coals until bread is golden brown and cooked through; turn every minute while cooking (individuals can hold their sticks as you sit around the campfire, or you can use a metal grate).

If inside of dough is not cooking, cover bread with foil and continue cooking.

Baste with butter and roll in plate of desired topping.

A MORSEL OF BREAD

A picnic is where we let bread
wrap the rest of the food.

CHAPTER 56

Worshipers with Bread

*Then you will go on further from there, and you will come as far as
the oak of Tabor, and there three men going up to God at Bethel
will meet you, one carrying three young goats, another carrying
three loaves of bread, and another carrying a jug of wine.*

I Samuel 10:3

MY GRANDMOTHER ALWAYS HAD A SNACK ready for my cousins
and me anytime we visited. Our home also stayed prepared for cousins,
aunts, or other people to drop in. With thirteen cousins who lived within
three houses either side of us, that meant lots of visitors. My mother
always kept the breadbox and cookie jar filled. She taught me to cook and
keep the breadbox supplied as well.

Guests felt welcomed because we were always prepared to pause from
our activities, sit with them, and provide something to eat and drink. My
mother often sent guests off with a plate of food and a greeting to family
members who had not accompanied them.

When I faced cold winters up north alone, enterprising kids would come by to shovel snow. I'd warm up bread and cookies and take them out to feed the young workers. Neighborhood children also came when I held an open house for chocolate or pretzel making. They took home plates full of goodies they made.

Greeting people with something fresh and homemade shows you invested time in preparing for company. Part of generosity is being prepared with something to give to others. It's also a willing spirit that wants to sprinkle joy into the lives of other people and doesn't expect anything in return. We give because God has blessed us.

LOVIN' FROM THE LORD

They will greet you and give you [Saul] two loaves of bread,
which you will accept from their hand.

1 SAMUEL 10:4

Saul went on a hunt for his father to find their lost donkeys. He searched without success, so his servant suggested they consult a man of God. Saul was concerned that he had no bread to offer the servant of God but decided he could offer a gift of silver instead.

Meanwhile, God had told the prophet Samuel that He was sending a man to be king. As Saul arrived, God told Samuel, "This is the man" (1 Samuel 9:17 NIV).

Saul found Samuel and asked where he could find the prophet. Samuel introduced himself and announced that the donkeys had been found and he had news for Saul. Samuel anointed Saul and gave him instructions. He prophesied that Saul

---

FOOD FOR THOUGHT

How have you seen God's sovereignty?

How do you see God's plan in the birth of Jesus?

---

would meet three men going to worship God who would be carrying three goats, three loaves of bread, and some wine. The men would give Saul two loaves of bread, and the Spirit of the Lord would come upon Saul. He would become a new man, changed by the Spirit. This all happened, and then Saul became king. God had chosen him.

God prepared the men with the bread for Saul and orchestrated the meeting. God used a gift of bread as part of the sign for Saul. God chose three men bearing three gifts: goats, bread, and wine. God often uses three as a reflection of the Trinity. These items were used in sacrifice, and God sent them to confirm Saul as king. The wise men who visited Jesus also bore three gifts for the newborn King: gold, frankincense, and myrrh.

Our sovereign God puts plans in motion and uses signs when needed to confirm His choices and plans.

LOVIN' FROM THE OVEN

TRINITY ROLLS

Any bread dough can be used to make Trinity rolls, including the Honey-of-an-Egg Whole Wheat Bread in this book (after the dough has risen and been punched down; see page 33).

Directions

Pull apart dough and make 1-inch balls. Place three balls in each well of a greased muffin tin. Let rise 20 minutes.

Bake at 350°F for 15–20 minutes or until golden brown.

They bake together as one roll, but have three separate sections, to symbolize the Trinity.

A MORSEL OF BREAD

Bread uses all the senses
to help us be aware
of our surroundings.

CHAPTER 57

Royal Feast

"He has brought me to his banquet hall,
and his banner over me is love. Sustain me with raisin cakes,
refresh me with apples, because I am lovesick."
Song of Solomon 2:4–5

MY HUSBAND AND I spent a morning on a British ship as special guests. My husband was stationed on the Coast Guard barque *Eagle*, the tall ship that would lead the parade of ships into New York Harbor for a celebration the following week. I had flown to Bermuda to meet him in port and arrived in time for Bermuda's celebration of Queen Elizabeth's birthday.

The British Navy ship was decked out with all its flags flying. They escorted us around the ship and then to a special reception on the bow. They served English tea and biscuits. Scones, teacakes, and other delicacies filled several trays. We sat and munched as we watched the parade and listened to the bands playing. We stood for the song, "God Save the Queen." I felt honored to be a guest for such a royal occasion. I also enjoyed listening to the sailors speak about their country and loyalty to the monarchy. They had such a sense of pride and honor in serving their country and queen.

There's something special about a tea—dressing up, enjoying bread, biscuits (cookies to us in the United States), and tea. It reminds me that someday in heaven we will *all* enjoy a royal banquet. We are children of the King, our heavenly Father. Until that day, however, we can honor God here and share our loyalty and pride in an awesome God.

LOVIN' FROM THE LORD

David said unto him, Fear not: for I will surely shew thee kindness
for Jonathan thy father's sake, and will restore thee all the land of Saul
thy father; and thou shalt eat bread at my table continually.

2 Samuel 9:7 KJV

David became king and remembered his friend, Jonathan. He asked if anyone remained of Jonathan's family and learned that one crippled son named Mephibosheth had survived. David sent for him and invited him to eat at his table. David treated him like his own sons and made sure he received the income from land that had belonged to his father and grandfather.

FOOD FOR THOUGHT

Do you ever feel unworthy to receive God's love?

How can you see your life as a banquet served by the King?

It surprised Mephibosheth, who had felt overlooked and unworthy. David cared for him and brought him to the banquet table as an honored quest. He became a loyal friend to David, grateful for being chosen.

In the Song of Solomon, the bride describes the joy of being invited to the king's table and receiving fruit and bread cakes. She is honored and in love with the king.

These glimpses into royal banquets remind us that there will be a great banquet, the wedding feast of Jesus and His bride, the church. It will be a time of great rejoicing and grateful hearts.

THE JOY OF BREAD MAKING

I helped my grandmother bake bread in coffee cans and package them to send to missionaries. Some wrote back to say they'd had a feast from what she mailed, or they had enjoyed it at teatime.

Years later, with a husband in the military and other relatives also serving, I often mailed treats, including homemade goodies. One time I sent cookies, with two each wrapped in plastic wrap. The mail delays and crushing of the package ended up turning the foam cooler into packing material. Jim laughed that he was thankful I had used the plastic. He could unwrap each packet of crumbs and eat them, and they still tasted good.

Tips for Mailing Bread

- Plan to pack and mail the same day you bake the bread or other goodies.
- Bread baked in coffee cans travels well. Leave it in the can and add the lid after the bread completely cools.
- Let bread cool on the counter. Hot bread releases steam in a package, and that causes sogginess.
- For soft breads, place them in a sealed, freezer-quality plastic bag.
- For hard-crusted breads, place in a foil-lined bag and then into a plastic bag.
- Squeeze air out of the bags.
- Place bread in center of shipping box and line the outside with popped corn, wadded newspaper, or bubble wrap to prevent movement. It's good to also cushion the bottom and top of box. Ideally, add two to three inches of cushion all around the bread.

Write *perishable* on outside of package.

- Next-day shipping is best so it will arrive fresh.
- It's better to ship breads in cooler months.

A MORSEL OF BREAD

Tea with scones or biscuits
makes a marvelous break in the day.

CHAPTER 58

Promised Long Ago

Then to Adam He said, "Because you have listened
to the voice of your wife, and have eaten from the tree
about which I commanded you, saying,
'You shall not eat from it;' cursed is the ground because of you;
in toil you will eat of it all the days of your life.
Both thorns and thistles it shall grow for you;
and you will eat the plants of the field."

Genesis 3:17–18

WE HELD AN OLD TESTAMENT BIBLE STUDY in our home for singles in the military. They couldn't commit to bringing refreshments or when they might show up, so that left me to cook weekly. To avoid growing weary or feeling resentful, I challenged myself to make each session special. I decided to match the week's study with food from that period of history.

It became a joy to cook, and the people arrived wondering what I had found to match the readings. I learned to make hamentashen with poppy seed filling when we studied Esther, fig cakes when we learned about King David, and other foods to accompany various readings. One evening, only one person showed up. She apologized and asked if we would still have the study.

Jim said, "God sent you, so yes, we will." At the end, I gave her leftover bread to share at work. She felt so overwhelmed with gratitude and thankful that we had cared enough to continue with just her that she called everyone from the study, as well as other friends, to share what the evening had meant to her. The next week, the house overflowed. When we work with a joyful heart and focus on God's call, He will bless the effort.

LOVIN' FROM THE LORD

And I will put enmity between you and the woman,
and between your offspring and hers;
he will crush your head, and you will strike his heel.
GENESIS 3:15 NIV

After casting Adam and Eve out of the garden, God cursed the ground, causing man to work hard for bread and to depend on God for the rain needed for growth. Repeating the phrase "you will eat" three times in Genesis 3:17–19, God emphasized the hard work to produce food, named as bread in verse 9. As he worked and sweated, Adam became the first breadwinner and discovered the cost of a broken relationship with God.

God, however, in His great wisdom, already had a plan, a promise for which He used the farming term of *seed*. Springing to life within the womb of a woman, the seed would be part of a family. The prophecy

FOOD FOR THOUGHT

What amazes you about God's promises?

What helps you focus on promises from God?

of the seed referred to Jesus and came with a word about sowing and earning bread.

Eve's offspring, her seed, would crush or bruise the serpent's head, even though the serpent would strike the heel of the offspring. Similar terms *crush* and *bruise* are used for milling wheat into flour. How interesting that even as man worked crushing grain, it could be a reminder of God's promise of restoration. From the greatest tragedy and act of disobedience came the greatest promise of restoration for all people.

That promise spanned many generations, but when Jesus came, many rejected Him. He didn't come as an earthly king, yet He multiplied bread to show His power over the earth and His ability to supply food.

THE JOY OF BREAD MAKING

Keeping Bread Fresh

- Fresh bread should not be stored in the refrigerator. If it will not be eaten in a few days, it is better to freeze it. The coldness of the refrigerator causes the starch in the bread to crystalize. That causes the bread to dry out and ruins the texture.
- Bread is best wrapped in cloth or placed in a cloth bag. Bread placed in a paper bag dries out quickly. Cloth allows moisture to exit, although that means the bread will mold quicker. That's why it needs to be eaten in a day or two. Wrapping a clean, dry kitchen towel around the bread will work too.
- Plastic keeps bread soft, like sandwich slices. The sealed bag traps the moisture and that's what keeps it soft. That's not so good for crusty breads, breadsticks, or baguettes.
- To freeze bread: Cool completely. Then wrap the bread well in freezer-grade plastic wrap (that will be moisture- and vapor-proof material) and add an outer layer of foil. When ready to use the bread, thaw at room temperature. This can take three hours.

A MORSEL OF BREAD

People, like batter in muffin cups,
only need to be half filled.
God will cause each one to rise up
and become more than expected.

CHAPTER 59

Give Thanks

And He said to them, "I have earnestly desired
to eat this Passover with you before I suffer."

LUKE 22:15

FRIENDS HAVE OFTEN INVITED ME to Seder dinners, and I enjoy them. It's a glimpse into what Jesus celebrated at Passover. One of my favorite times was taking my younger children to the home of Messianic friends, where they took time to set it up and explain each part of the meal and all the various foods.

Jerry and Marlon graciously welcomed us and involved the children, especially our youngest son. Every part of the meal is symbolic and reveals truths about God; it also shares history of the Jewish people. The meal celebrates the gratitude of the people that God had delivered them from slavery in Egypt.

Three pieces of matzo (unleavened bread) are placed in a stack. The middle one is called the afikomen. It is broken in two during the beginning of the meal, and one half is wrapped in a napkin and hidden. Children hunt for the hidden piece to receive a reward.

For Christians, it also celebrates the night that Jesus gave us a new covenant and new tradition with bread and wine. Some scholars think the bread Jesus broke was the afikomen. Jesus is like unleavened bread, revealed as He broke bread. That is reflected in the road to Emmaus account when the two walking with Jesus did not recognize Him until He had broken bread with them. The drinking of the cup of redemption is the cup Jesus called His blood. It's the third cup of the Seder meal.

We are grateful now that God delivered us from slavery to sin.

LOVIN' FROM THE LORD

While they were eating, Jesus took bread,
and when he had given thanks, he broke it and gave it
to his disciples, saying, "Take and eat; this is my body."
MATTHEW 26:26 NIV

Communion is celebrated differently in various denominations, but it always centers on what Jesus did at the Last Supper. It is sometimes called the *Eucharist*, a Greek word for thanksgiving, because Jesus gave thanks and then broke the bread.

God wants to be with us. In the Old Testament, God required showbread to be set on the altar as part of the covenant with the Israelites. The offerings of grain and the display of showbread reflected the covenant relationship with God and laid a foundation for understanding Jesus as the Bread of Life. At the heart of feasting together, from early times to the Lord's Supper, is community and the ultimate promise of a communal banquet prepared for believers in heaven.

FOOD FOR THOUGHT

When has God multiplied your gratitude?

How do you feel when you break bread with others?

One theme of bread in the Bible is covenant relationship with God. A covenant is a spiritual agreement or promise that includes a relationship with God. Jesus said He gave us a new covenant when He broke the bread.

After receiving, we, as disciples, should go out with compassionate and grateful hearts and give to those who hunger but do not come. A hymn sung in many churches, called "Awake, Awake to Love and Work," includes the words, "To give and give again, what God hath given me." That phrase reminds us to pass along our blessings.

Eucharist begins with the miracle of Jesus giving Himself, but it continues when we, in turn, give to others. The miracle of multiplying continues in our hearts, and that is part of the wonder of breaking bread as Christians.

LOVIN' FROM THE OVEN

As my daughter Darlene's family celebrates the Passover and then the Last Supper, followed by the death and resurrection of Jesus, her children love finding empty eggs. They hunt for empty plastic eggs and yell, "The tomb is empty, and Jesus is risen!" Then they enjoy eating sparkling resurrection rolls with colorful insides.

SPARKLING RAINBOW
RESURRECTION ROLLS

Ingredients
    Crescent rolls or refrigerated biscuit dough
    Large marshmallows (1 for each roll)
    Candy sprinkles

Directions
    Heat oven to 400°F. Open rolls and flatten biscuit dough.
    Sprinkle dough with candies. Place a marshmallow on each roll and close dough over it, sealing it well.

Bake 10 minutes until golden brown.

The rolls will be empty inside, and the wall will be lined with color from the candies.

A MORSEL OF BREAD

Jesus gave us a lasting gift of bread.
He is a giver who always
has more to give.

CHAPTER 60

Extravagant Love

May there be abundance of grain in the earth on top
of the mountains; its fruit will wave like the cedars of Lebanon;
and may those from the city flourish like vegetation of the earth.

PSALM 72:16

WHEN I LIVED IN THE MIDWEST, the endless fields of wheat covering the plains always reminded me of Psalm 72, which describes an abundance of grain. The shining stalks reveal the wealth of the land and God's blessings, as reflected in the song, "America the Beautiful." During famines, grain is much more valuable than silver or gold. Grain is a blessing.

One of my friends shared a custom from her childhood. She grew up in Oklahoma, where they greeted newcomers with fresh-baked bread. She called it "breading newcomers." Each day, for a whole week, someone baked and gave the new family a loaf of bread. That's an extravagant welcome and blessing, especially as she experienced it during the Great Depression when food was scarce.

God is excessive too and wants us to visualize endless satisfaction. Bread multiplied in both the Old and New Testaments reflects extravagance.

God loves us extravagantly and desires to give us an abundant life of blessings.

LOVIN' FROM THE LORD

When [the people] were filled, [Jesus] said to His disciples,
"Gather up the leftover fragments so that nothing will be lost."
JOHN 6:12

Feeding five thousand people with only two fish and five loaves of bread revealed God's ability to give so much when given so little. It is a sign of His ability to feed us spiritually. Yet, what happened after this miraculous meal is often overlooked.

After the meal, Jesus told the disciples to gather the remains. The broken pieces of bread filled twelve baskets! Our omniscient God could have provided the exact amount needed, but He provided much more.

All four gospels relate this event, but not one tells us what happened to the leftovers. Jesus made only one comment: "Let nothing be wasted" (NIV). Soon after this event, the disciples climbed into a boat, apparently without the twelve cumbersome baskets of bread.

> ### FOOD FOR THOUGHT
>
> How has God lavished you with love?
>
> When your heart is hungry, do you turn to God to satisfy your hunger?

The number of baskets matches the number of disciples. Jesus left the choice of what to do with the food to the disciples. Jesus only highlighted the need to gather it up and use it. In Eucharist, we, as disciples, still face the same choice the disciples did after their bounteous meal.

In receiving from Jesus, the Bread of Life, we receive a great abundance, more than enough spiritual food for ourselves. The choice of what to do with what we receive is up to each of us as individuals. Jesus provided food, not to show power but, in His own words in Mark 8:2, "I feel compassion for the people because they have remained with Me now three days and have nothing to eat."

Jesus, in His compassion, wanted to satisfy them not just one time, but always. He later disclosed this in His sermon about Himself as the Bread of Life in John 6. Jesus showed us extravagant giving. In Revelation 3:20, He asks us to open the door of our heart to let Him in and promises to dine with us. He will be our wholesome bread to satisfy our heart. Jesus is ready to satisfy all hungry hearts because there is no limit to His love and extravagant giving.

LOVIN' FROM THE OVEN

I make these as breakfast biscuits for company. The citrus smell is a great morning scent, and using oranges goes with living in Florida.

ORANGE CHOCOLATE CHIP BISCUITS
FOR A CROWD

Ingredients

14 cups biscuit mix

4 tablespoon fresh grated orange peel

3 cups milk

1 cup orange juice

1 package chocolate chips

Directions

Heat oven to 400°F. Mix all ingredients to make soft dough. Turn onto a floured surface and knead for 1 minute.

Divide in half. Roll to half-inch thickness, forming a 10x10-inch square. Cut into 2-inch squares. Place close together on ungreased baking sheet. Bake for 8–10 minutes until lightly browned.

Makes 50 biscuits.

A MORSEL OF BREAD

Share what you have,
even a slice of bread,
and you will be blessed.

Conclusion

Give, and it will be given to you. They will pour into your lap
a good measure—pressed down, shaken together, and running over.
For by your standard of measure it will be measured to you in return.

LUKE 6:38

JESUS USED TERMS RELATED TO GRAIN when He encouraged people to be generous. This verse refers to boundless generosity where the grain overflows, shaken to let out air to make room for the real kernels.

In the marketplace, merchants would fill a container with grain. The buyer would stomp on it and press it down to get rid of the empty air. Then they would shake it. This compressed it to make room for more, to get a full measure.

God wants to bless us additionally in response to how we bless others. Into the lap, or a pouch formed by a garment, reflects the idiom of something beneficial arriving unexpectedly. And for us to "fall into the lap of luxury" is a reflection of the blessing spoken about in this verse.

Generosity is God's currency. A grain can be planted to produce much for a great harvest. Being generous plants a seed that God nurtures and grows to give us a future harvest.

Generosity touches hearts and blesses people in many ways. Blessing someone is a gift of encouragement. Christ showed us generosity in giving so much to us. He gave us hope for the future and showed us that giving to others brings them hope. The Bread of Life gave us a principle regarding generosity to put in practice and reflect upon when we enjoy bread, make bread, break bread, and give bread to others.

NOTES

Chapter 11

1. George Washington, *The Writings of Washington*, ed. John C. Fitzpatrick (Washington, DC: Government Printing Office, 1932), 15:55. From Washington's speech to the Delaware Indian Chiefs on May 12, 1779.

Chapter 33

1. "The Orphans Who Survived the Nazi Camps," http://news.bbc.co.uk /2/hi/uk_news/8597635.stm. Accessed March 13, 2017.

Chapter 43

1. Benjamin Franklin and William Temple, *Memoirs of the Life and Writings of Benjamin Franklin* (London: Colburn, 1818), 19.

Acknowledgements

Bread baking has been part of my life from childhood. I am deeply grateful to my agent Mary G. Keeley's faith in finding a home for the book. Thanks to Pamela Clements at Worthy who saw the vision for the book.

I am also thankful for my friends through the years who shared the joy of bread, including cadets at the US Coast Guard Academy and midshipmen at the US Naval Academy who tested and ate my bread for years.

I am thankful for my friend Ellen Lelasher who shared years of making breads and crafts as we entered our wares in fairs and made them as gifts for others. I relish the memories of bread with Janet Gonski who enjoyed the bread and watching our late husbands (Jim and Ron) feast on hot bread weekly during their grad school years. Barbara Hale and Anne Stoppe, you have also enjoyed chatting with me as I wrote the book and recalled past memories. I am thankful for my children who had fun making bread with me from their early years and still enjoy the breads I make (Rebecca, Michael, James, Darlene, and Daniel). I am also thankful to have twelve grandchildren who enjoy bread making and feasting on bread.

Each book needs some support during the writing process, so thanks to my fellow prayer warriors in the AWSA mastermind group and my church Faith and Fellowship group for tasting the breads as I checked each recipe and took photos.

ABOUT THE AUTHOR

KAREN WHITING is an international speaker, former television host, and award-winning author of twenty-five books for women, children, and families. She has a heart to help families thrive and build strong, wholesome bonds. She has written more than seven hundred articles for more than sixty publications and loves to let creativity splash over the pages of what she writes. Currently, Karen writes for Leading Hearts, The Kid's Ark, and Molly Green Magazines.

As a Coast Guard wife, Karen lived in many states, almost always near the water. She has a degree in mathematics, and is a widow, mother of five, including two rocket scientists (yes, for real) and a grandmother. Her writing awards include the Christian Retailing Best Award, children's nonfiction (*The One Year My Princess Devotions*) and the Military Writer's Society of America Gold Medal (*Stories of Faith and Courage from the Home Front*).

Karen serves on the board of directors of Christian Authors Network where she helps other published authors promote books to book lovers everywhere.

She likes adventure and has ridden a camel in the Canary Islands; white water rafted in Australia; ridden horseback in the ocean in Jamaica; and enjoyed scuba diving off the coast of Bermuda. She's spoken in such far away places as Russia and Malaysia. Her travels and moves helped her appreciate many varieties of breads and foods. She loves to bake and gift others with homemade bread, muffins, and other baked goodies.

Visit Karen online at karenwhiting.com.

IF YOU ENJOYED THIS BOOK, WILL YOU CONSIDER SHARING THE MESSAGE WITH OTHERS?

Mention the book in a blog post or through Facebook, Twitter, Pinterest, or upload a picture through Instagram.

Recommend this book to those in your small group, book club, workplace, and classes.

Head over to facebook.com/worthypublishing, "LIKE" the page, and post a comment as to what you enjoyed the most.

Tweet "I recommend reading #TheGiftOfBread by @karenhwhiting // @worthypub"

Pick up a copy for someone you know who would be challenged and encouraged by this message.

Write a book review online.

Visit us at worthypublishing.com

twitter.com/worthypub

worthypub.tumblr.com

facebook.com/worthypublishing

pinterest.com/worthypub

instagram.com/worthypub

youtube.com/worthypublishing